# THE SHROUD OF TURIN

## A CASE FOR AUTHENTICITY

*"He is the image of the invisible God."* —Colossians 1:15

# THE SHROUD OF TURIN

## A CASE FOR AUTHENTICITY

Fr. Vittorio Guerrera

*"For God, who commanded the light to shine out of darkness, hath shined in our hearts, to give the light of the knowledge of the glory of God, in the face of Christ Jesus."*

—2 Corinthians 4:6

TAN BOOKS AND PUBLISHERS, INC.
Rockford, Illinois 61105

ISBN 0-89555-680-4

Library of Congress Control No. 00-134501



Cover illustration: The entombment of the body of Christ in the Shroud, by Jean Gaspard Baldoino (1590-1669). Original located in the Chapel of the Holy Shroud, Nice, France. Photo courtesy of Confrérie de la Très Sainte Trinité/Penitents Rouges de Nice.

Printed and bound in the United States of America.

TAN BOOKS AND PUBLISHERS, INC.
P.O. Box 424
Rockford, Illinois 61105
2001

# CONTENTS

# ACKNOWLEDGMENTS

The author would like to thank the following individuals for their assistance with this book: Evelyn Fracasso, Ph.D., Fr. William Donovan, and Fr. William Henn, O.F.M. Cap., for proofreading the manuscript and for editorial suggestions; Fr. Thomas Buffer, Fr. Hans Hintermaier and Rachel Wisler for their proficiency with foreign languages; Fr. Joseph Marino, O.S.B. and Charles Coretto for bibliographical references; and Jack Orabona for his computer graphic skills.

# PREFACE

> Peter then came out with the other disciple, and they went toward the tomb. They both ran, but the other disciple outran Peter and reached the tomb first; and stooping to look in, he saw the linen cloths lying there, but he did not go in. Then Simon Peter came, following him, and went into the tomb; he saw the linen cloths lying, and the napkin, which had been on his head, not lying with the linen cloths but rolled up in a place by itself. Then the other disciple, who reached the tomb first, also went in, and he saw and believed.
>
> —*John* 20:3-8

FROM that day onward, the course of human history changed because of what those disciples saw and believed when they peered into that empty tomb. Even though the Gospels relate that only the linen cloths were present and that the body of Jesus was nowhere to be found, many believe that the disciples saw more than just the burial cloths. They also saw the imprint of the crucified body of Jesus Christ on the Shroud. Ever since that day, the story of the Shroud's travels has been filled with intrigue and legend. Reports of the Shroud or what has been likened to the Shroud have been circulated in Turkey, Constantinople, France, and eventually Italy. The Shroud, which has been preserved in the Cathedral of Turin since 1578, is believed by many to be that very same cloth.

The Shroud has been the object of devotion for many centuries. Popes, princes and peasants have traversed far and wide to pray before this mysterious image. Although the Roman Catholic Church has never officially declared the Shroud of Turin to be the authentic burial cloth of Jesus Christ, she has permitted its veneration by the faithful. The Church's faith in the Resurrection of Christ does not rest upon the authenticity of the Shroud, but on the witness of the Apostles. As St. Paul teaches, "Faith then comes by hearing, and hearing by the word of Christ" (*Rom.* 10:17).

In 1988, the Church allowed radiocarbon dating to be conducted on the Shroud to obtain an age for the cloth. This test was long awaited by believers and nonbelievers alike. If the Shroud dated back to the first century, that would uphold its authenticity. If not, nonbelievers would rejoice that it was a forgery. The test yielded a medieval date. Skeptics were pleased, while believers were dismayed. For some, this datum put to rest the story of the Shroud. However, those who were convinced of the Shroud's authenticity remained undaunted and forged ahead with research. Although the Church has not permitted any further scientific testing of the Shroud to date, independent and interdisciplinary research continues.

In this book I have attempted to unfold the drama of the Shroud. It is my conviction, based upon the evidence presented here, that the Shroud of Turin is the authentic burial cloth of Jesus Christ. While it is beyond the scope of science to identify with certitude the man on the Shroud, I am hopeful that the reader will come to weigh the evidence and decide in favor of this case for authenticity.

# THE SHROUD OF TURIN

## A CASE FOR AUTHENTICITY

*"The Lord bless thee, and keep thee. The Lord show his face to thee, and have mercy on thee. The Lord turn his countenance to thee, and give thee peace."* —Numbers 6:24-26

## –1–

# History of the Shroud

THE Shroud of Turin is a linen cloth of ivory color measuring fourteen feet three inches long by three feet seven inches wide or eight cubits long by two cubits wide, according to first-century Jewish measurements. (A cubit is equivalent to 21.7 inches.) The cloth is made of a three-to-one herringbone weave with a "Z" twist. Parallel to one side of the cloth is sewn a six-inch-wide strip of the same weave pattern. It is generally believed that this piece was added to the Shroud in order to insert a rod to facilitate its exposition. The Shroud bears the frontal and dorsal image of a naked, crucified, bearded man, approximately five feet eleven inches tall, between the ages of 30-35, weighing about 175 pounds. Many people believe that this Shroud is the burial cloth of Jesus Christ.

The history of the Shroud can be traced with assurance to the mid-fourteenth century. Prior to that period, little is known with absolute certainty concerning its whereabouts. A third century Syrian text mentions a cloth that is associated with the miraculous cure of King Abgar V, ruler of Edessa (13-59 A.D.), now called Urfa, in southeastern Turkey. This story was translated almost verbatim by Eusebius, bishop of Caesarea, in his *Ecclesiastical History* in 325 A.D.[1] According to the story, Abgar suffered from an ailment, perhaps leprosy. Having heard about the healing powers of Jesus, he sent a certain Ananias around the year 31-32 A.D. with a letter to Jesus requesting that He come and heal him. Jesus replied that He was unable to go, but promised to send one of His disciples. It was not until after His death and Resurrection that one of the seventy-two disciples, Thaddeus, brought a cloth to Abgar bearing an image of the face of Jesus. Upon seeing this cloth, Abgar was cured, and the Christian Faith was established in the city. (Actually, the first Christian king of Edessa was Abgar VIII, who ruled from 177-212.) Although the Syrian text mentions a cloth, for reasons unknown, Eusebius makes no reference to it; rather, he states that Abgar saw a vision when he looked at Thaddeus. "Immediately on his entrance there appeared to Abgar a great vision on the face of the Apostle Thaddeus. When Abgar saw this, he did reverence to Thaddeus, and wonder seized all who stood about, for they themselves did not see the vision, which appeared to Abgar alone."[2]

While the Syrian account refers to Thaddeus as one of the seventy-two disciples of the Lord (cf. *Luke* 10:1), he soon came to be associated with Jude Thaddeus, the apostle who was a cousin of Jesus (cf. *Matt.* 13:55; *Mark* 6:3). One of the earliest Byzantine icons to depict Thaddeus holding the Image of Edessa, as the cloth was referred to there, was painted in 550 A.D. and is located at St. Catherine Monastery on Mount Sinai. In the Western tradition, St. Jude is often represented holding an image of the face of Jesus over his heart. It has been suggested by the British historian Ian Wilson that the Image of Edessa was actually the Shroud folded in such a way that only the face was visible. Early replicas of the Image were portrayed as an elongated trellis frame with a circle in the middle that depicted the face. A sixth-century text called *The Acts of Thaddeus* refers to such an image as a *tetradiplon*, a Greek word which literally means "doubled in four" or, put another way, folded in eight layers.[3] Interestingly, this Greek word is not used for any other object. Dr. John Jackson, an Air Force physicist who was part of the 1978 Shroud of Turin Research Project, "found that doubling the cloth in four did indeed expose the face area. Furthermore, Jackson found an eight-fold pattern of folds. . . ."[4]

After the death of King Abgar V, his son Man'nu reverted to paganism and persecuted the Christians of Edessa. At that time the cloth disappeared. Most likely it was hidden for safekeeping, and was not seen again for five hundred years. During the centuries that followed the disappearance of the cloth, Edessa suffered intermittent floods, the most devastating one taking place in 525 A.D. when the river Daisan flooded the city. According to a contemporary writer, Procopius of Caesarea, extensive damage was done to buildings, and many were destroyed. "It levelled to the ground a large part of the outworks and of the circuit-wall and covered practically the whole city, doing irreparable damage. For in a moment it wiped out completely the finest of the buildings and caused the death of one third of the population."[5] The future emperor Justinian (527-565), nephew of the aged Justinian I, quickly dispatched engineers to rebuild the city. According to popular tradition, the cloth was found in a niche above Edessa's west gate during the reconstruction of a wall.[6] The reason for the historical silence concerning this discovery could be due to the fact that "Edessa was predominantly Monophysite in A.D. 525, and it is difficult to envisage this faction welcoming the discovery of a relic that seemed to confound their beliefs."[7] (Monophysitism is the heretical concept that Jesus had only one nature, i.e., the divine. As such, Monophysites would be opposed to any physical representation of Christ.)

The cloth was later placed in a chapel of the new

Cathedral of Hagia Sophia, where it was kept in a reliquary. When the city was threatened during the Persian siege under King Chosroes Nirhirvan in 544 A.D., the citizens of Edessa brought out the Image, and the attackers retreated. This story can be found in the writings of the Syrian historian Evagrius (527-600).[8] It was he who first referred to the cloth as *acheiropoietos* ("not made by human hands").

The relic managed to survive during the turbulent period of the iconoclast controversy of the eighth and ninth centuries, when Emperor Leo III (714-741) issued a decree calling for the destruction of all religious icons as being idolatrous and heretical. The Catholic Church never condoned iconoclasm, but rather condemned it. Pope Stephen III spoke in favor of the use of sacred images in a Lateran synod in 769.[9] Later, in 787, the Second Council of Nicea endorsed the veneration of images, and particular mention was made of the Image of Edessa as being one "not made by human hands."[10] It was referred to as one of the main arguments by the Fathers of the Church to defend the legitimacy of the use of sacred images.

The story of how the Image came to Constantinople is rather peculiar. It is said that in 943, the Byzantine Emperor Romanus Lecapenus requested that the cloth be brought to him to protect his city from enemy invasion. He sent General John Curcuas to Edessa with a proposition for the emir. In exchange for the famous relic, Lecapenus offered 12,000 pieces of silver, the release of 200 Moslem prisoners, and the promise that Edessa would be spared attack.[11] Needless to say, it was an offer the Moslem ruler could not refuse.

When the cloth arrived in Constantinople on the Feast of the Dormition (or Assumption) of the Blessed Virgin Mary on August 15, 944, it was received in the church at Blachernae. The cloth was referred to as the "Mandylion," coming from an Arabic word which means "veil" or "handkerchief." The name first appears about the year 990 in a biography of the Greek ascetic, Paul of Mt. Latros, in which it is stated that he was given a vision of the icon.

A tenth-century Byzantine writer relates that on the evening of the Mandylion's arrival in Constantinople, Emperor Romanus Lecapenus, his two sons and future son-in-law Constantine, who was a young boy at the time, had a private showing of the Image. According to Constantine, the Image was a "moist secretion without colors or the art of a painting."[12] Another author, Symeon Magister, writing about the same time, said that the Emperor's sons were disappointed because they were only able to distinguish a faint image of a face on the cloth.

There is extant a Greek manuscript discovered by Dr. Gino Zaninotto in 1986 of a sermon given on August 16, 944 by Gregory, archdeacon and administrator of Hagia Sophia Cathedral, where the Mandylion was placed by the Ecumenical Patriarch Theophylartos for the veneration of the faithful.[13] There it was crowned with the imperial crown and placed on the Emperor's throne to show the sovereignty of Christ the Pantocrator. In his sermon, Gregory exhorts: "The splendour—and may everyone be inspired by this description—was impressed during the agony only by the drops of sweat that poured forth from the face which is the source of life, dropping down like drops of blood, as from the finger of God. These are really the beauties that have produced the colouration of the imprint of Christ, which was further embellished by the drops of *blood that issued of His own side*"[14] [emphasis added]. This is convincing evidence that the Mandylion was not simply a cloth bearing the image of the face of Christ, but that it was the Shroud folded as a *tetradiplon*.[15]

Some Orthodox Christians contend that the Shroud and the Mandylion are not one and the same. Their main objection is that the Mandylion shows the live face of Jesus, whereas the Shroud depicts a dead Jesus. One reason for this seeming discrepancy may be due to the fact that the early Christians were reluctant to portray a dead Christ. Since the Shroud was rarely displayed full-length, when artists made copies of the Holy Face from the Mandylion, they portrayed Christ with His eyes open. We do find that, as early as the sixth century, many facial features found on the Shroud are reproduced in paintings. Artists often depicted the face in a frame surrounded by an ornamental trellis. If the Mandylion were indeed the Shroud folded in such a way so that only the face was exposed, it would be natural to depict Jesus alive with His eyes open. According to Fr. Edward Wuenschel C.Ss. R., one of the pioneer historians of the Shroud, realistic representations of the crucifixion did not become common until the thirteenth century, and even then, mainly in the Western Church.[16]

One year after the Mandylion was brought to Hagia Sophia, in 945, Byzantine Emperor Constantine Porphyrogenitos commissioned a hymn to be composed which recounted the history of the Mandylion. This emperor established August 16, the anniversary of the solemn exposition of the cloth, as the Feast of the Holy Mandylion in the Orthodox Church. It is said that in 1011 a replica of the Mandylion was sent to Rome, where it became known as the "Veil of Veronica," and that Pope Sergius IV had an altar consecrated for it in the chapel of Pope John VII in St. Peter's. The appellation of the "Veil of Veronica" to the Mandylion is itself shrouded in legend. According to pious tradition, when Jesus was making His way to Calvary, a woman of Jerusalem offered Him her veil to wipe the sweat and blood from His face. After she had pressed it against His face, she noticed that His image was imprinted on the cloth. This scene is depicted in the sixth station of the Way of the Cross. Although the New Testament does not relate this account nor make any mention of this woman's name, tradition gives her the name "Veronica." This name derives from two Latin/Greek words: *vera*, meaning "true," and *eicona*, meaning "likeness" or "image." Therefore, the Veronica is a "true image" of the Holy Face. Another copy of the Veil of Veronica is venerated in the Church of St. Bartholomew of the Armenians in Genoa. This was reportedly given to a Genoese captain, Leonardo Mantaldo, by Byzantine Emperor John V Palaelogos in 1362.

Following the solemn exposition on August 16, 944, the Mandylion was moved to the Pharos Chapel in the Boucoleon Palace and rarely displayed. Testimonies from the eleventh and twelfth centuries attest to its presence in Constantinople. In 1080, Alexis I Comnenus implored the aid of Emperor Henry IV and Robert of Flanders in defending "the linens found in the tomb after his Resurrection."[17] Other distinguished leaders who saw the Mandylion were King Louis VII of France in 1147, Bishop William of Tyre, and King Amaury of Jerusalem in 1171.

Nicholas Mesarites, the custodian of the cloth kept in the Pharos Chapel, described how he had to defend the relics against a mob in a palace revolution in 1201. He writes: "In this chapel Christ rises again, and the sindon with the burial linens is the clear proof. . . . The burial sindon of Christ: this is of linen, of cheap and easily obtainable material, still smelling fragrant of myrrh, defying decay, because it wrapped the mysterious, naked, dead body after the Passion. . . ."[18]

In 1204, Constantinople was sacked during the Fourth Crusade led by Boniface, the Marquess of Montferrat. For three days the brutish warriors, most of whom were Frenchmen, mercilessly attacked Christians in the city. They stole gold, silver and sacred relics. Robert de Clari, a knight from Picardy, took part in the capture of the city, which ultimately fell on April 12, 1204. He chronicled the events in his diary, *La conquête de Constantinople*. In it, he relates how he saw various holy relics, but what impressed him the most was the cloth at Blachernae: "There was another of the churches which they called My Lady St. Mary of Blachernae, where was kept the sydoine in which Our Lord had been wrapped, which stood up straight every Friday so that the figure of Our Lord could be plainly seen there."[19]

After the conquest of Constantinople, de Clari notes, "And no one, either Greek or French, ever knew what became of this sydoine after the city was taken."[20] The Mandylion disappeared for about 150 years until it reappeared in Lirey, France in the 1350s. One theory advanced to explain the silence of these missing years is that of Ian Wilson. He claims the cloth was probably in the possession of a religious order of knights known as the Knights Templars. They were founded around 1118 by two French knights, Hugh of Payens and Geoffrey of Saint-Omer, and seven of their companions. They were originally known as the Poor Knights of Christ of the Temple of Solomon, because they were headquartered near the ruins of Solomon's Temple. These men took vows of poverty, chastity and obedience. Their purpose was to defend the sacred sites in the Holy Land, and they took part in all but the first of the ten Crusades between 1095 and 1291. Oftentimes, princes and nobles would entrust them with their treasures and religious artifacts for safekeeping. There is some circumstantial evidence that the Mandylion was sold by Baldwin II, the last of the Latin Byzantine Emperors, to St. Louis IX, King of France, in return for a loan.[21]

The Templars were a somewhat mysterious group. It was alleged that they worshipped a "head" in their secret ceremonies. On October 13, 1307, they were suppressed in France by order of King Philip IV the Fair and Pope Clement V. A couple of the Grand Masters, namely Jacque de Molay of France and Geoffrey de Charny of Normandy, were burned at the stake on March 19, 1314 on the small island called *Ile des Javiaux* facing the Cathedral of Notre Dame.

The theory that the Templars may have possessed the Shroud is supported by the discovery in 1944 of a painting of the Holy Face (circa 1280) on a wooden panel in the village of Templecombe, England. This village was owned by the Knights Templars from about 1185. Rex Morgan, a Shroud scholar, hypothesized that the wooden panel may actually have been a lid to a wooden box which contained the Shroud when it was transferred from France to England during the suppression of the Templars.[22] "The Templecombe panel has 125 points of congruence with the Shroud face . . . The fleur-de-lis decoration of the painting strongly suggests French influence and the quatrefoil design is recurrent in Templar . . . decorative motifs."[23] The theory is very plausible, except that the Templars never admitted to possessing the Shroud.

The only city to have claimed to possess the Shroud from 1208 to 1329 was the French city of Besançon. The theory is that during the Fourth Crusade, the Burgundian knight who commanded the district of Blachernae where the Shroud was kept, Othon de la Roche, Duke of Athens and Sparta, received it as part of his recompense. The claim that the Shroud was in Athens is attested to directly in a letter by Theodore of Epirus dated August 1, 1205, and indirectly by Nicholas of Otranto, abbot of the monastery of Casole. Othon, in turn, sent the cloth to his father, Ponce de la Roche, who then handed it over to the Bishop of Besançon, who placed it in the Cathedral of St. Etienne where it was exposed for veneration each year on Easter until 1349. In that year a fire burned down the Cathedral causing slight damage to the Shroud. In the midst of all the confusion, the Shroud disappeared. According to a dubious sixteenth-century account kept in the second church of Lirey, the Shroud was given to King Philip VI. He subsequently gave it to a friend whose name, coincidentally, was the same as the Templar Grand Master who was burned at the stake, Geoffrey I de Charny!

De Charny was captured by the English after the Battle of Calais in 1349 and sent to England as a prisoner of war. It is conjectured that he may have concealed the Shroud in Templecombe. He remained in England until 1351, when King John II of France paid for his release. In June 1353, King John granted de Charny permission to build a collegiate church in Lirey. In a letter dated May 28, 1356, Henri of Poitiers, Bishop of Troyes from 1353-1370, writes:

> Henri, by the grace of God and of the Apostolic See, confirmed bishop elect of Troyes, to all those who will see this letter, eternal salvation in the Lord. You will learn what we ourselves learned on seeing and hearing the letters of the noble knight Geoffrey de Charny, Lord of Savoy and of Lirey, to which and for which our present letters are enclosed, after scrupulous examination of these let-

> ters and more especially of the said knight's sentiments of devotion, which he has hitherto manifested for the divine cult and which he manifests ever more daily. And ourselves wishing to develop as much as possible a cult of this nature, we praise, ratify and approve the said letters in all their parts — a cult which is declared and reported to have been canonically and ritually prescribed, as we have been informed by legitimate documents. To all these, we give our assent, our authority and our decision, by faith of which we esteem it our duty to affix our seal to this present letter in perpetual memory.
>
> Given in our palace of Aix of our diocese in the year of Our Lord 1356, Saturday, the 28th of the month of May.[24]

Although there is no mention of a Shroud in this letter, the bishop congratulates de Charny on his "devotion . . . for the divine cult" and his own wish to "develop as much as possible a cult of this nature." The repeated references to this cult could only refer to the sacred object housed in the church and not the church proper, thereby suggesting that the Shroud was in Lirey by 1356. This document, which is kept in the archive of Aube, Lirey, is the only genuine act of Bishop Henri de Poitiers that can be authenticated.

During this same year a painted copy bearing only the frontal image was displayed in the church of Besançon, since the faithful had become accustomed to venerating it there. The historian Dom Chamard noted that the shroud exhibited in Besançon after 1352 was merely a replica. He further noted:

> Dunod in his *History of the Church of Besançon* speaks of the Shroud preserved in the Cathedral of

> St. Etienne (Besançon) in the thirteenth century, and proceeds thus: "In March, 1349, the church was destroyed by fire, and the box in which the Holy Shroud was kept, seemingly without much formality, was lost. Some years afterwards the relic was found again by happy chance, and to make sure that it was the same as was formerly venerated in the church of St. Etienne, it was laid upon a dead man, who immediately revived. The fact of this miracle is established not only by the records of the church of Besançon but also by a manuscript preserved up to the present time in the church of St. James, at Rheims, where it has been placed by Richard La Pie, senior priest of Besançon, in the year 1357, who has been himself an eye-witness."[25]

Dunod does not state that the original Shroud was returned to Besançon. The copy kept at Besançon was eventually destroyed in 1792 during the French Revolution.[26]

Geoffrey de Charny died in the Battle of Poitiers on September 19, 1356. His widow, Jeanne de Vergy, who was the great-great-great-great granddaughter of Othon de la Roche, then acquired the cloth. Being in financial straits after the death of her husband, she began to exhibit the Shroud in 1357 to raise money for the upkeep of the church. On June 5, 1357, twelve bishops gathered to sign a grant of indulgences to pilgrims who visited the collegial church at Lirey.[27] For reasons unknown, Jeanne de Vergy and her son, Geoffrey II de Charny, who coincidentally was married to Marguerite de Poitiers, the niece of Bishop Henri, waited some thirty years before attempting to display the cloth again.

By 1389 Jeanne had remarried, and her husband Aymon of Geneva was the uncle of the anti-pope Clement VII, who reigned from 1378-1394 in Avignon during the

Western schism. Jeanne and her son circumvented obtaining permission from the new Bishop of Troyes, Pierre d'Arcis, by appealing directly to the anti-pope's legate, Cardinal Pierre de Thury.

The opening of the exhibition in April 1389 generated such a furor that the bishop had recourse to Clement VII. The anti-pope responded by confirming his permission and imposing silence on the bishop. Not satisfied, the bishop appealed to King Charles VI to revoke his permission for the exhibition, but to no avail. In exasperation, Bishop d'Arcis wrote his famous *Memorandum* to Clement VII. In it he charged:

> The case, Holy Father, stands thus. Some time since in this diocese of Troyes the Dean of a certain collegiate church, to wit, that of Lirey, falsely and deceitfully, being consumed with the passion of avarice, and not from any motive of devotion but only of gain, procured for his church a certain cloth cunningly painted, upon which by a clever sleight of hand was depicted the twofold image of one man, that is to say, the back and front, he falsely declaring and pretending that this was the actual shroud in which our Saviour Jesus Christ was enfolded in the tomb. . . . The Lord Henry of Poitiers, of pious memory, then Bishop of Troyes, becoming aware of this, and urged by many prudent persons to take action, as indeed was his duty in the exercise of his ordinary jurisdiction, set himself earnestly to work to fathom the truth of this matter. For many theologians and other wise persons declared that this could not be the real shroud of our Lord having the Saviour's likeness thus imprinted upon it. . . . Eventually, after diligent inquiry and examination, he discovered the fraud and how the said cloth had been cunningly painted,

> the truth being attested by the artist who had painted it, to wit, that it was a work of human skill and not miraculously wrought or bestowed. Accordingly, after taking mature counsel with wise theologians and men of the law, seeing that he neither ought nor could allow the matter to pass, he began to institute formal proceedings against the said Dean and his accomplices in order to root out this false persuasion. They, seeing their wickedness discovered, hid away the said cloth so that the Ordinary could not find it, and they kept it hidden afterwards for thirty-four years or thereabouts down to the present year.[28]

Bishop d'Arcis' letter accuses the clergy of Lirey with simony and alludes to the so-called investigation made by his predecessor, but he does not substantiate the charges he levels. One would think that if the artist admitted to painting the image, he would have written a confession. As it is, there is no record of any confession nor the name of the alleged artist. Also, if one were to subtract "thirty-four years" mentioned in d'Arcis' letter from 1389, the year in which it was written, that brings us to 1355, which predates the benevolent letter of Bishop Henri of Poitiers of 1356 and the indulgences granted to pilgrims in 1357. Yet, opponents of the Shroud's authenticity often refer to this letter as historical proof that the Shroud is a medieval forgery. D'Arcis even admits that "although it is not publicly stated to be the true shroud of Christ, nevertheless this is given out and noised abroad in private, and so it is believed by many, the more so because, as stated above, it was on the previous occasion [i.e. in 1356/57] declared to be the true shroud of Christ. . . ."[29]

In the 1900s, Ulysee Chevalier, a French medieval scholar who denied the Shroud's authenticity based upon this memorandum, found himself transcribing the following quote from a period text: "Extract that I have made from a Latin piece undated that appears to be a letter or request from a bishop of Troyes or another ecclesiastic to a pope."[30] Father Luigi Fossati, S.D.B., a sindonologist (one who studies the Shroud) and professor at the Salesian Institute in Turin, has said: "The document seemed to be only a rough draft never put in final form to be sent to the Pope. Even Chevalier defines it as a pro-memoria."[31] The letter was never sent, which may account for the lack of the usual title for an official document. The title, *Memorandum of Pierre d'Arcis*, was appended by those who discovered this letter.[32] Nicholas Camuzat (1575-1655), canon and archivist of the diocese of Troyes, does not even mention this *Memorandum* in his *Promptuarium Tricassinae Diocesis*, where he makes specific reference to the church of Lirey and to Bishops Henri de Poitiers and Pierre d'Arcis.[33]

The anti-pope Clement VII never ordered an investigation into the accusations made by Bishop d'Arcis. In a bull dated January 6, 1390, he authorized the continuation of the exposition of the Shroud, provided it was presented as an image or likeness of Christ and not as the true Shroud: "Under no circumstances should the ecclesiastics wear hooded cape, rochet, alb, or cope, nor should they perform other solemnities that are customary when exposing relics for which neither torches, flambeaux nor candles are lighted, nor should any other lamps be used."[34] He further ordered the bishop not to oppose its exposition.

When Geoffrey II de Charny died on May 22, 1398, his daughter Margaret de Charny became the owner of the Shroud. Two years later she married Jean de Baufremont. Their marriage ended tragically when Jean was killed at the Battle of Agincourt in 1415, leaving Margaret childless. In 1418, a war broke out in the vicinity of the chapel, and the clergy asked Margaret's second husband, Humbert de Villersexel, to protect it in his castle of Montfort near Montbard. Humbert acknowledged receiving the relic in a letter dated July 6, 1418. In it he wrote:

> During this period of war, and mindful of ill-disposed persons, we have received from our kind chaplains, the dean and chapter of Our Lady of Lirey, the jewels and relics of the aforesaid church, namely the things which follow: first a cloth, on which is the figure or representation of the Shroud of our Lord Jesus Christ, which is in a casket emblazoned with the de Charny crest. . . . The aforesaid jewels and relics we have taken and received into our care from the said dean and chapter to be well and securely guarded in our castle at Montfort.[35]

Humbert also stipulated in his letter that these objects would be returned to the clergy of Lirey after the war. When Humbert died in 1438, however, Margaret guarded the Shroud jealously, taking it with her wherever she traveled.

After the war was over, the clergy at Lirey requested on May 8, 1443 that Margaret return the Shroud. Perhaps fearing its future fate, as the church in Lirey had fallen into disrepair, Margaret refused, even enduring threats of excommunication. On March 22, 1453, she gave it to her cousin Anna, the daughter of the King of Cyprus and wife of Duke Louis I of Savoy, who was a descendant of St. Louis IX, King of France. Margaret died seven years later on October 7, 1460.

The Savoy dynasty was founded in 1003 and ruled Savoy and the Piedmont region, which extended from southeastern France across the Alps to northwestern Italy. The family was noted for their piety and they associated with a number of Franciscan friars. The Duke built an ornate chapel in Chambery, the Savoy capital in France, a town about fifty miles east of Lyons. On February 6, 1464, Duke Louis gave fifty francs to the clerics of Lirey as recompense for their loss of the Shroud's possession.

After the death of Duke Louis, his son Amadeus IX succeeded him as duke. In 1471, at the age of sixteen, Amadeus IX began to enlarge and embellish the chapel. The newly renovated chapel was inaugurated on June 11, 1502 by Duke Philibert II. At that time the Shroud was placed in a silver reliquary above the high altar, closed by an iron grate and locked with four keys.

On Good Friday, April 14, 1503, the Shroud was displayed in the city of Bourg-en-Bresse in honor of Archduke Philip the Fair's safe return from Spain. His sister, Margaret of Austria, was married to Duke Philibert II. Antoine de Lalaing, secretary to Philip the Fair, tells of how one of the three bishops holding the Shroud for veneration solemnly announced: "Here, my brothers, among holy things, is the most holy and contemplative on all the earth. It is the precious and noble 'sindon' purchased by Joseph of Arimathea for the burial of the divine Master, when, with the help of Nicodemus, he took him down from the cross."[36] Lalaing continues: "To prove if it was the true Shroud, it was boiled in oil, tossed in fire, laundered different and numerous times. But one could not efface nor remove these imprints and marks of our sweet Lord."[37] There is a certain degree of doubt as to whether or not this actually took place, because Lalaing does not mention that he was an eyewitness. The thought of the Shroud being subjected to such a trial is horrifying, but in medieval times such treatment was considered a legitimate truth detector test.

Tragedy struck on December 4, 1532 when fire broke out in the sacristy of the chapel and made its way to where the Shroud was kept. The intensity of the heat was such that molten silver dripped from the cover of the reliquary and penetrated the folded Shroud. Two Franciscan friars, Guglielmo Pessod and Francesco Lambert, ran into the chapel to retrieve the Shroud and doused the chest with water. The fire was extinguished, and the precious relic was saved. The parallel set of burn marks that runs down the entire length of the cloth is a reminder of that fire. From April 15 to May 2, 1534, the Poor Clare nuns of Chambery repaired the burnt parts of the Shroud by applying a number of triangular patches.

In 1537 when French troops invaded, the Shroud was taken to Vercelli and then to Nice. In 1549, the cloth was returned to Vercelli, but on November 18, 1553, the French sacked the city, and the Shroud was hidden in the house of Antoine Claude Costa, one of the canons. On June 3, 1561 the Shroud was returned to Chambery and exposed for the first time on August 15, 1561.

Emmanuel Philibert, the Duke of Savoy, brought the Shroud to Turin, Italy on September 14, 1578. One of the principal reasons for doing so was so that St. Charles Borromeo might venerate it. The saint had been the first resident archbishop of Milan in more than eighty years. During a plague that was devastating northern Italy, he vowed to make a pilgrimage to venerate the Shroud in return for Milan's deliverance from the plague. Although only forty years old, Borromeo was sickly, and to spare him the arduous journey to Chambery, the Duke of Savoy brought the Shroud closer to him. The other reason for bringing the Shroud to Turin was that the duke had plans to move his capital there. A month after the Shroud's arrival on October 10, Charles Borromeo made his way into the city barefoot amidst a great deal of fanfare. The saint spent eight days in Turin venerating the Shroud. He was to make two other pilgrimages to the Holy Shroud before he died in the year 1584.

The Shroud was never returned to Chambery and was exposed for veneration each year on the 4th of May in front of the Palazzo Madama. Some of the other saintly personages who made pilgrimages to the Shroud were St. Francis de Sales in 1613 and St. Jane Frances de Chantal in 1639. In writing to his mother in 1614, Francis de Sales recalls his pilgrimage to Turin:

> Annecy, 4 May 1614
>
> Whilst waiting to see you, my very dear Mother, my soul greets yours with a thousand greetings. May God fill your whole soul with the life and death of His Son Our Lord!
>
> At about this time, a year ago, I was in Turin, and, while pointing out the Holy Shroud among such a great crowd of people, a few drops of sweat fell from my face on to this Holy Shroud itself. Whereupon, our heart made this wish: May it please You, Saviour of my life, to mingle my unworthy sweat with Yours, and let my blood, my life, my affections merge with the merits of Your sacred sweat!
>
> My very dear Mother, the Prince Cardinal was somewhat annoyed that my sweat dripped onto the Holy Shroud of my Saviour; but it came to my heart to tell him that Our Lord was not so delicate, and that He only shed His sweat and His blood for them to be mingled with ours, in order to give us the price of eternal life. And so, may

our sighs be joined with His, so that they may ascend in an odour of sweetness before the Eternal Father.

But what am I going to recall? I saw that when my brothers were ill in their childhood, my mother would make them sleep in a shirt of my father's, saying that the sweat of fathers was salutary for children. Oh, may our heart sleep, on this holy day, in the Shroud of our divine Father, wrapped in His sweat and in His blood; and there may it be, as if at the very death of this divine Saviour, buried in the sepulchre, with a constant resolution to remain always dead to itself until it rises again to eternal glory. We are buried, says the Apostle, with Jesus Christ in death here below, so that we may no more live according to the old life, but according to the new. Amen.

Francis, Bishop of Geneva
The 4th of May 1614[38]

On June 1, 1694, the Shroud was placed in a chapel of the Cathedral of St. John the Baptist designed by the abbot, Guarino Guarini. Except for a brief period during World War II, it has been kept there ever since. In 1939, Cardinal Maurilio Fossati, Archbishop of Turin, secretly moved the Shroud for safekeeping to the Benedictine Abbey of Montevergine located at Avellino, about 140 miles south of Rome. There it remained until it was returned to Turin in 1946. That year the last Duke of Savoy, King Umberto II, was deposed. He died in Geneva on March 18, 1983. In his will he bequeathed the Shroud to the Holy See, but the Pope left the relic in the custodial care of the Archbishop of Turin.

Since its transferral from Chambery to Turin, the Shroud has been on public display twenty-three times, on the following occasions:[39]

1585: wedding of Charles Emanuel I and Catherine of Augsburg, daughter of King Philip II of Spain.
1586: birth of Philip Emanuel, first child of Charles and Catherine
1587: baptism of Vittorio Amedeo I
1613: in honor of St. Francis de Sales
1620: wedding of Vittorio Amedeo I and Maria Cristina of Bourbon-France
1639: visit of St. Jane Frances de Chantal (foundress of the Visitation sisters)
1722: visit of the Cardinal of Acunia
1736: visit of Prince Constantine and Cristina Enrica of Assia
1737: on May 4 for the feast of the Holy Shroud
1750: wedding of Vittorio Amedeo III and Maria Antonietta of Bourbon-Parma
1798: departure of Charles Emanuel IV for Sardegna
1804: visit of Pope Pius VII on November 13 on his way to France
1814: return of Vittorio Emanuel I to Turin
1815: return of Pius VII on May 21, following his release from exile by Napoleon the previous year
1822: by order of Charles Albert
1841: wedding of Vittorio Emanuel II and Maria Adelaide of Augsburg
1868: wedding of Prince Umberto and Margaret of Savoy. Repairs to the cloth were made by Princess Clotilde of Savoy while working on her knees.
1898: the Italian kingdom's fiftieth anniversary
1931: wedding of Prince Umberto and Maria Jose of Belgium
1933: Holy Year commemorating 1900th anniversary of the death and Resurrection of Jesus Christ

1978: on the occasion of the 400th anniversary of the Shroud's transferral to Turin
1998: on the occasion of the 500th anniversary of the Cathedral and the centennial anniversary of the first photograph taken by Secondo Pia
2000: Holy Year commemoration of the birth of Jesus Christ

It was during the exposition of 1898 that Secondo Pia, a Turin lawyer and amateur photographer, was given permission by King Umberto I to photograph the Shroud. From May 25-28, 1898, he took various exposures of the Shroud. As the wet plates were being developed, he was amazed to discover that the negative photographic image was in actuality a positive picture of a crucified man. He would later describe his experience: "Shut up in my darkroom all intent on my work, I experienced a very strong emotion when, during the development, I saw for the first time the Holy Face appear on the plate, with such clarity that I was dumbfounded by it. It was a great glory and I was seized by trepidation at what I had seen."[40]

Marquis Fillipo Crispolti was the first to make the discovery public. On June 13, 1898, he wrote: "The picture makes an indelible impression . . . the long and thin face of Our Lord, the tortured body and the long thin hands are evident. They are revealed to us after centuries, nobody having seen them since the Ascension into Heaven."[41]

From May 2-23, 1931, the Shroud was exhibited for the first time in the twentieth century on the occasion of the wedding of Prince Umberto of Piedmont. During that time it was photographed once again with better equipment by the photographer Giuseppe Enrie at the request of Cardinal Fossati. Among those present was Secondo Pia. Enrie's photographs were clearer than those taken by Pia and soon became circulated throughout the world. From that point on, the Shroud has generated research and controversy among believers and skeptics alike.

## –2–

# Popes and the Shroud

THROUGHOUT the centuries popes have issued statements and/or have paid homage to the Shroud of Turin. The following is a listing of some of the most notable.

Pope Stephen III (768-772), shortly after his election, wrote in a homily concerning the Shroud: "[He] stretched his whole body on a cloth, white as snow, on which the glorious image of the Lord's face and the length of his whole body was so divinely transformed that it was sufficient for those who could not see the Lord bodily in the flesh to see the transfiguration made on the cloth."[1]

Pope Sergius IV (1009-1012) consecrated an altar to the Mandylion or the Veronica in the chapel of Pope John VII located in the basilica of St. Peter in 1011.[2]

Pope Paul II (1464-1471) granted Duke (Blessed) Amadeus IX permission to construct a collegiate church at Chambery "for the preservation of certain most precious relics"[3] and assigned twelve canons in 1467.

Pope Sixtus IV (1471-1484) issued four bulls indicating that he believed in the authenticity of the Shroud.[4] He gave the chapel of Chambery the title *Sainte Chapelle* or the "Holy Chapel of the Holy Shroud," granting it numerous privileges and indulgences. Before becoming a cardinal, Francesco della Rovere was a Franciscan theologian. In 1464 he wrote a paper called "The Blood of Christ," which was published in the second year of his pontificate. In it he said that "the Shroud in which the body of Christ was wrapped when he was taken down from the cross . . . is now preserved with great devotion by the Dukes of Savoy, and it is colored with the blood of Christ."[5]

Pope Julius II (1503-1513), a nephew of Sixtus IV, issued a bull on April 25, 1506, *Romanus Pontifex*, in which he approved an Office and Mass for the Holy Shroud for the canons of the *Sainte Chapelle* at Chambery. The feast of the Holy Shroud was to be celebrated on May 4, the day following what was then celebrated as the Feast of the Finding of the True Cross. The Pope solemnly pronounced:

> We, therefore, who by divine disposition, albeit unworthily, preside over the ministry of the sacred apostolate, considering that, if we adore and venerate the Holy Cross on which Our Lord Jesus Christ was suspended and by which we are redeemed, it surely seems fitting and binding upon us to venerate and adore the Shroud on which, as is reported, there are clearly seen the traces of the Humanity of Christ to which the Divinity had united itself, that is, (there is seen) His very Blood. . . . (We) approve and confirm the aforesaid day and night office of the Shroud together with its proper Mass.[6]

Pope Leo X (1513-1521) on October 17, 1514 extended the feast with its proper Mass and Office to all of Savoy.

Pope Clement VII (1523-1534), the legitimate pope who took the same name as the anti-pope to annul its usurpation by the former, confirmed the Feast of the Holy Shroud.

Pope Gregory XIII (1572-1585) extended the feast in 1582 to the entire House of Savoy, from southeastern France across the Alps to northwestern Italy. He also granted a plenary indulgence to all who visited the Shroud when it was exposed in that year.

Other popes who extended the feast, revised the text of the Mass and Office of the Holy Shroud and/or granted indulgences are: Pope Paul V (1605-1621), Pope Urban VIII (1623-1644), Pope Innocent X (1644-1655), Pope Alexander VII (1655-1667) and Pope Clement IX (1667-1669).

Pope Clement X (1670-1676) granted a plenary indulgence to the faithful who made a pilgrimage to the Shroud "not for venerating the cloth as the true Shroud of Christ, but rather for meditating on his Passion, especially his death and burial."[7]

Subsequent popes who approved or fostered devotion to the Shroud include: Pope Innocent XI (1676-1689), Pope Alexander VIII (1689-1691), Pope Innocent XII (1691-1700), Pope Clement XI (1700-1721), Pope Innocent XIII (1721-1724) and Pope Benedict XIII (1724-1730).

Pope Benedict XIV (1740-1758), speaking of other pontiffs' attitudes regarding the Shroud, said that they "have testified that the most notable relic of the Holy Shroud kept in the city of Turin is that same shroud in which the Lord Jesus Christ was wrapped."[8]

Other popes who also promoted the veneration of the Shroud were: Pope Pius VII (1800-1823), Pope Gregory XVI (1831-1846) and Pope Pius IX (1846-1878).

Pope Leo XIII (1878-1903) granted special indulgences for the exposition in 1898. He later wrote to Cardinal Richelmy, Archbishop of Turin, to express his gratitude at the number of people who had traveled from all parts of the world "to venerate the sacred Shroud of Christ."[9]

Pope St. Pius X (1903-1914) approved the *Oeuvre St. Luc* (Work of St. Luke), founded by Emanuel Faure, for the purpose of promoting devotion to the image of Christ as revealed on the photo of the Holy Shroud.[10]

Pope Pius XI (1922-1939) had an avid interest in the Shroud and collected historical and scientific information on the relic. When the Archbishop of Turin expressed to the Pope strong opposition from various quarters to cancel a planned exposition in 1931, the Pope replied: "You may be at peace. . . . We speak now as a scholar and not as Pope. We have made a personal study of the Shroud, and We are convinced of its authenticity. Objections have been made, but they are worthless."[11] In a radio address on December 24, 1932 and in his encyclical, *Quod Nuper*, of January 1, 1933, Pius XI expressed his desire that the relics of the Passion and death of Jesus Christ be exposed for veneration during the Jubilee year 1933, commemorating the nineteenth centenary of the Redemption. He told Cardinal Fossati of Turin privately that he had the Shroud specifically in mind.[12] On September 5, 1936, he received in audience a group of young men who belonged to Catholic Action and who were returning from a pilgrimage to the shrine of Our Lady of Pompeii. He handed them pictures of the Holy Face from the Shroud and said:

> These are pictures of her Divine Son, and one may perhaps say the most thought-provoking, the most beautiful, the most precious that one can imagine. They come precisely from that object which still remains mysterious, but which has certainly not been made by human hands. . . . that holy thing is still surrounded by considerable mystery; but it certainly is something more sacred than anything else. . . .[13]

Pope Pius XII (1939-1958), in a radio address to the National Eucharistic Congress held at Turin on September 13, 1953, said that the city "guards as a precious treasure the Holy Shroud, upon which we behold with deep emotion and solace the image of the lifeless Body and the broken Divine Countenance of Jesus."[14]

Pope John XXIII (1958-1963) received in audience on February 16, 1959 the *Cultores Sanctae Sindonis* of Turin and a group of devotees of the Holy Face from Ariola, Benevento. He told them of his fond memories of his many visits to Turin where he had the privilege of celebrating the Sacrifice of the Mass at the altar of the Holy Shroud.[15]

Pope Paul VI (1963-1978), in a television broadcast of the Shroud on November 23, 1973, said:

> We personally still remember the vivid impression it made on Our mind when, in May 1931, We were fortunate to be present on the occasion of a special celebration in honor of the Holy Shroud. Its projection on a large, luminous screen and the face of Christ represented thereon appeared to Us so true, so profound, so human and divine, such as We have been unable to admire and venerate in any other image. It was for Us a moment of singular delight.
>
> Whatever may be the historical and scientific judgment that learned scholars will express about this surprising and mysterious relic, We cannot but wish that it will lead visitors not only to deep sensitive observation of the exterior and mortal features of the marvelous figure of the Savior, but also introduce them to a more penetrating vision of His hidden and fascinating mystery.[16]

Pope John Paul I (1978) was elected pontiff in the same hour that the Cardinal of Turin was offering Mass to inaugurate the opening of the exposition of the Shroud (August 26-October 8).[17]

As a newly ordained priest in 1947, Fr. Karol Wojtyla (the future Pope John Paul II) paid a visit to Turin and prayed before the altar where the Shroud was kept in its reliquary.[18] Some thirty years later, as Archbishop of Krakow, Cardinal Wojtyla made another pilgrimage to Turin on September 1, 1978 following the election of Pope John Paul I. Little did he know that six weeks later he would be elected Supreme Pontiff after the untimely death of his predecessor. On April 13, 1980, John Paul II made his first pilgrimage to Turin as pope. In his homily he said:

> The Paschal mystery has found here some splendid witnesses and apostles, in particular from the 19th and 20th centuries. It could not be otherwise in this city which guards an unusual and mysterious relic as the Holy Shroud, a singular witness—if we accept the arguments of many scientists—of Easter: of the Passion, death and Resurrection. It is a silent witness, but at the same time surprisingly eloquent![19]

The Holy Father commented on his pilgrimage to Turin the following Sunday, April 20, before praying the *Regina Caeli* at St. Peter's: "The Cathedral of Turin: the place where is found, for centuries, the sacred Shroud, the most splendid relic of the Passion and of the Resurrection."[20]

While traveling to Madagascar on April 28, 1989, the Pope was asked by Orazio Petrosillo, one of the journalists aboard his flight, if he thought the Shroud was a relic or an icon, and the Pope replied: "It certainly is a relic!"[21] The Holy Father returned to Turin again on May 24, 1998 when the Shroud was exposed for a period of two months to celebrate the 500th anniversary of the Cathedral and the centennial of the first photograph taken by Secondo Pia. The Pope remarked that "the imprint left by the tortured body of the Crucified One . . . stands as an icon of the suffering of the innocent in every age."[22]

## –3–

# Scripture and the Shroud

WE know from the Gospels that after the body of Jesus was taken down from the Cross, it was wrapped in a linen cloth. The Synoptic Gospels use the Greek word *sindōn* to describe this Shroud (cf. *Matt.* 27:59; *Mark* 15:46; *Luke* 23:53). The Fourth Gospel, on the other hand, uses the word *soudárion* to refer to the cloth which covered the head of Jesus (*John* 20:7) and the plural *othónia* (*John* 19:40), often interpreted to mean "strips of linen," "wrappings" or "linen bandages." An entry in a biblical dictionary, however, states: "Nowhere in the account of Christ's burial is mention made of κειριαι, strips of cloth, bandages, such as bound the hands and feet of Lazarus in the tomb"[1] (*John* 11:44). According to one biblical scholar, this is a relatively modern interpretation. "Frequently, in koine Greek, diminuitive forms do not have a truly diminuitive force . . . and it is even questionable that *othónion* is a diminuitive, for *othónē* may designate the material and *othónion* may denote an article made of that material. . . ."[2]

The Aramaic word *soudara* refers to a small sweat cloth such as a handkerchief or napkin. This term seems to be used in a broad sense in Sacred Scripture. In the book of *Exodus*, after Moses had come down from Mount Sinai with the tablets of the Ten Commandments, his face had become radiant, for he had spoken with God. Thereafter, he would cover his face with a veil. The

Palestinian Targum (Aramaic paraphrase of the Old Testament) translates the Hebrew word for veil (*masweh*) as *soudara*. On the other hand, the book of *Ruth* mentions her being asleep at the feet of Boaz, wrapped in a mantle. Rather than using the Hebrew word *mitpachat* for mantle, the Targum pseudo-Jonathan uses the Aramaic *soudara* (*Ruth* 3:15), into which Boaz put six measures of barley the following morning. If the *soudara* were simply a handkerchief it would seem doubtful that it would be able to hold such a quantity of barley. In another context, in the book of *Jeremiah*, the prophet writes that the Lord instructed him to buy a linen girdle to wear (*Jer.* 13:1). The Hebrew word for linen girdle (*ezor*) is translated as *soudára* in the Syriac text. Eventually this Aramaic word was translated into the Greek *soudárion* and into the Latin *sudarium*.

In the Old Testament the *sindōn* was used for a variety of purposes other than for burial. Samson promised his companions "thirty linen tunics, [Hebrew: *s^edhīnīm*, Greek: *sindónas*] and as many coats" if they would solve a riddle for him (*Jdg.* 14:12). Interestingly, the Latin manuscript *Codex Vaticanus*, in lieu of *sindónas*, uses the word *othónia*, thereby indicating that the words were considered synonymous. The book of *Proverbs* speaks of the ideal wife who makes fine linen (*sindónas*) and sells it (*Prov.* 31:24). The word *sindōn* is also used in the New Testament to refer to the cloth worn by the young man who followed Jesus from a distance after His arrest in the Garden of Gethsemane. "There was a young man following him, who was covered by nothing but a linen cloth. As they seized him he left the cloth behind and ran off naked" (*Mark* 14:51-52).

It would seem, then, that the Greek word *soudárion* as used by John is equivalent to *sindōn* and *othónia* for the other wrappings used in burial. To complicate matters a little more, Luke, who had previously used the word *sindōn* before the Resurrection (*Luke* 23:53), refers to the *othónia* found in the tomb after the Resurrection (*Luke* 24:12). The word *othónia*, therefore, can refer to collective cloths of various sizes. Evidence to support this theory can be found in a fourth century inventory made by a Roman government official who was making his way from upper Egypt to Antioch around the year 320 A.D. Under the heading of *Othónia* he listed a number of linens, including four *sindónes* and two types of handkerchiefs.[3]

## Jewish Burial Customs

According to the *Mishnah*, a collection of oral laws first codified by Rabbi Judah around 200 A.D., the first step in the burial process was to wash the body with warm water and to anoint it only if the limbs are not moved (*Shabbat* 23:5). The fact that bodies were washed after death is indicated in the book of *Acts* where it records the death of the convert Tabitha in Joppa: "At about that time she fell ill and died. They washed her body and laid it out in an upstairs room." (*Acts* 9:37). On the other hand, there is no mention of washing the bodies of those, such as Ananias and Sapphira, who died a dishonorable death (*Acts* 5:6,10).

Whether or not the body of Jesus was washed is a matter of debate among scholars. A change in burial practice is reported to have been introduced between the time of Jesus and the *Mishnah*.[4] It seems unlikely that the body of Jesus was washed, for a number of reasons. First and foremost, no Gospel account mentions that it was done. Yet, this would have been the most basic service rendered one who died on a cross and was covered with blood. Secondly, "the Sabbath was about to begin" (*Luke* 23:54). That being the case, the disciples would not have had much time to do so, as work was prohibited on the Sabbath (cf. *Luke* 23:56). Also, according to Jewish law (*halachah*), there are four conditions which prohibit the body from being purified: if a Jew dies a violent and bloody death, if a Jew dies by capital punishment for a crime of a religious nature, if a Jew is an outcast of the Jewish community, or if a Jew is murdered by a Gentile.[5] Certainly all these conditions applied to Jesus. Wilson asserts that "Only on the view that Jesus was not washed can the authenticity of the Turin Shroud be upheld."[6]

Anointing and spices were customary elements for an honorable burial. These are not mentioned in the Synoptic accounts of Jesus' burial. In the Gospel of Mark the Evangelist writes: "And when the sabbath was past, Mary Magdalene, and Mary the mother of James, and Salome, bought sweet spices, that coming, they might anoint Jesus" (*Mark* 16:1). In Luke's version, after the burial "they prepared spices and ointments" (*Luke* 23:56). No reference to spices and ointments is made in the Gospel of Matthew. "That Jesus was anointed and embalmed before burial (without a hint that the process was incomplete) is not easily reconciled with the information in *Mark* and *Luke* (but not *Matthew*) that on Easter morning the women were coming to anoint Jesus."[7] The Fourth Gospel alone envisions an honorable burial for Jesus: "They took therefore the body of Jesus, and bound it in linen cloths, with the spices, as the manner of the Jews is to bury" (*John* 19:40).

Biblical scholars have divergent opinions as to whether or not the body of Jesus was anointed after being taken down from the Cross. "None of the Gospels posits that Jesus was anointed with oil between death and burial."[8]

According to Rabbi Dan Cohn-Sherbok of the University of Kent in Cambridge, England: "If this is correct, then it would be reasonable to conclude that washing did not take place either."[9] The four Gospels, however, do record a pre-anointing story (*Matt.* 26:6-13; *Mark* 14:3-9; *Luke* 7:36-50; *John* 12:3-8). Although there are significant differences among these four accounts, all the Evangelists with the exception of Luke record the anointing of Jesus by the woman at Bethany shortly before His Passion. If this anointing were merely a common gesture of hospitality, it is doubtful that this episode would have been recorded at all by each Gospel writer.

In Mark's Gospel the woman anticipates the burial rite of anointing by pouring the ointment over Jesus' head. The fact that she broke the jar indicates that she planned to use the entire contents. "She hath done what she could: she is come beforehand to anoint my body for the burial" (*Mark* 14:8). According to one scriptural exegete: ". . . anointing for burial was not her intent; that is how Jesus chose to see it."[10] By contrast, another scholar states that "the use of very expensive perfume shows that the woman's act does not follow the normal practice of hospitality."[11]

In John's Gospel the woman anoints Jesus' feet rather than His head (*John* 12:3). "Mary's action constituted an anointing of Jesus' body for burial. . . . One does not anoint the feet of a living person, but one might anoint the feet of a corpse as part of the ritual of preparing the whole body for burial."[12] Jesus says to those around Him: "Let her alone, that she may keep it against the day of my burial" (*John* 12:7). No mention is made that the jar was broken. "The Greek could mean that she was to keep ointment for a future burial, but v. 3 seems to indicate it was all used, as does Mark."[13]

Matthew's version is similar to that of Mark. Although

there is no mention of the breaking of the jar, the ointment is poured over Jesus' head. "For she in pouring this ointment upon my body, hath done it for my burial" (*Matt.* 26:12). The account of the women's attempt to anoint the body of Jesus after death is omitted in Matthew's Gospel, suggesting that the Evangelist was satisfied that this ritual had been done.

Luke does not record the anointing of Jesus by the woman at Bethany. Instead, he relates the story of the sinful woman who washes Jesus' feet with her tears, dries them with her hair, and then proceeds to perfume them with oil (*Luke* 7:38). There is no mention here by Jesus that this act anticipated His burial.

The most notable correlation between Jewish burial customs and the Shroud is the requirement to bury in a single sheet a person who was executed by the government.[14] The *Mishnah* also instructs that the eyes of the body have to be shut, and the chin has to be tied with a chin band (*Shabbath* 23:5). Evidence of a jaw band measuring approximately two inches wide can be seen on a three-dimensional image of the Shroud. "The hair of the man seems to be separated from the cheeks. The hair on the left side of the face hangs out over the edge of an object. . . ."[15] It has been postulated by some that the *sudarium* (sweat cloth, napkin) which had been on the head of Jesus was actually the chin band (*John* 20:7). "But here the expression is not as clear as in the account of Lazarus. . . . In *John* 11:44 the appropriate word (οψις—face) is used, but there it is said that the sweat cloth was bound *about his face*"[16] [emphasis added]. The cloth found in Jesus' empty tomb is referred to by the Gospel writer as that which was "*on his head*." In addition, "there is . . . in the Eastern tradition, before the days of the New Testament, the word *soudara*, which has not the same meaning as the classical Latin *sudar-*

*ium* and its Greek transcription *sudárion*, but refers to a full linen garment."[17] It would thus not seem likely that the *sudarium* would have been used as a chin band.

With regard to the protocol used to wrap the body of Jesus, the four Evangelists differ in their use of the Greek word to describe this procedure. For example, Matthew and Luke use the verb *enetylixen*, which means "to wrap" or "to fold" (cf. *Matt.* 27:59; *Luke* 23:53). Mark uses the word *eneilēsen*, coming from *eneiléō*, meaning "wrapped" or "confined" (cf. *Mark* 15:46). And John uses the verb *dein*, which means "to bind" or "tie" (*John* 19:40). When one hears the word "wrapped" in English, the image evoked is that of swathed mummies, but "there is no evidence that the Jews wrapped their corpses with bands or strips similar to those used for Egyptian mummies."[18] The literal sense of the Greek word means "to envelope."[19] The body of Jesus was laid on a single linen sheet that was drawn up the back and down the front of the body, and His limbs were bound. The image of the man on the Shroud of Turin shows signs that his legs were indeed tied. This would have been normal procedure. When Lazarus was raised from the dead, for example, the Gospel says that his hands and feet were bound (*John* 11:44). Another reason for tying the limbs could have been to help in the transport of the body to the tomb.

## Good Friday and the Shroud

*Jesus was scourged by Roman soldiers prior to His Crucifixion* (*Matt.* 27:26; *Mark* 15:15; *John* 19:1). The Shroud shows evidence of about 120 scourge marks, some visible only under ultraviolet light. The instrument used to cause these marks was likely the Roman *flagrum*, which was a whip constructed from two or three leather strips with two small balls made of lead or bone tied at each end. When a *flagrum* was used to whip a person, it would tear off pieces of flesh. The scourge marks on the man on the Shroud are "nearly always in clusters of twos or threes."[20] According to the Mosaic Law, 40 lashes were the maximum number of strokes allowed (cf. *Deut.* 25:3). Oftentimes the victim died from the scourging alone. To insure that they did not exceed the legal limit, the tormentors would give only 39 lashes (cf. *2 Cor.* 11:24). Roman executioners, however, were free to administer as many lashes as they wished since they did not adhere to the Mosaic law.[21] According to Dr. Pierre Barbet, who wrote his comprehensive work, *A Doctor at Calvary*, "there must have been two executioners. It is possible that they were not of the same height, for the obliqueness of the blows is not the same on each side."[22]

*Jesus was struck at the head and spat upon* (*Matt.* 26:68, 27:30; *Mark* 14:65, 15:19; *Luke* 22:63-64; *John* 18:22, 19:3). The image on the Shroud shows a bruised face, a broken nose and a swollen right eye that is almost closed.

*Jesus was crowned with thorns* (*Matt.* 27:29; *Mark* 15:17; *John* 19:2). The head of the man on the Shroud is covered with numerous puncture holes with blood trickling downward, which suggest a cap of thorns. This covered the entire head and was not just a circlet as is often depicted on a crucifix. According to Dr. Jackson, "these puncture-type wounds are consistent with thorns from a Jerusalem plant with vicious one to three-inch spikes."[23]

*Jesus was made to carry His Cross* (*John* 19:17). The Shroud image shows that the man must have carried a heavy object on his shoulders, for there are bruises and cuts on his shoulders and knees: "On the right shoulder . . . there is a broad excoriated area, which is in the form of a rectangle of about 10 x 9 centimetres.

. . . On the left side, there is another area of excoriations of the same type. . . . It is round, with a diameter of about 5½ inches."[24] These wounds demonstrate that the man likely carried a cross-beam or *patibulum*, rather than a full-length "T" cross. When the condemned man reached the place of crucifixion, the *patibulum* would have been attached to the vertical beam or the *stipes*, which was permanently fixed into the ground.

*Jesus was nailed to the Cross by His hands and feet* (cf. *Luke* 24:39-40; *John* 20:20-27; *Col.* 2:14). The image of the man on the Shroud reveals that he had been pierced through the wrists and feet. The right wrist is hidden under the left hand (in negative photo), and a blood flow can be seen coming from the base of the left hand. In traditional depictions of the Crucified Jesus, He is shown nailed through the palms, but Scripture does not specify this. Dr. Barbet states that this would have been scientifically impossible because the weight of the body would have torn the hand right through the nail. In Hebrew there is no word for "wrist," and the word *yad* was often used to refer to other parts of the hand.

The hand wound image on the Shroud depicts the exit of the nail, not its entrance, and thus the nail could very well have passed through the upper part of the palm, pointing toward the arm, emerging as shown on the Shroud. Dr. Frederick Zugibe, a pathologist, states that the upper part of the palm could easily have been supported the weight of the body and that this is the most plausible explanation. These two theories will be explored further in Chapter 8.

*His heart was pierced, and blood and water poured forth* (*John* 19:34). This was the final mortal blow inflicted upon the crucified man to ensure he was dead. The executioner would most likely have used a lance or short javelin he was carrying. According to tradition, this blow was thrust on the right side of the chest. Most believe that the heart is on the left, but "the heart is mesial [central] and in front, resting on the diaphragm, between the two lungs. . . . Only its point is definitely to the left, but its base extends to the right beyond the breastbone."[25] The Shroud shows evidence that the wound is indeed to the right, for there is a blood stain with a breadth of at least 2¼ inches that comes downwards, undulating and narrowing for about six inches:

> The greatest axis of this wound is just under two inches in length, while it has a height of about two-thirds of an inch. . . . The inner end of the wound is four inches below and a little to the outside of the nipples, on a horizontal line running just under four inches below it. . . . The lower and inner extremity of the wound runs horizontally slightly more than an inch below the point and is just under 4½ inches from the mesial line. The upper and outer extremity runs horizontally one-fifth of an inch below the point and is about six inches from the mesial line.[26]

Barbet speculates that the lance must have penetrated above the sixth rib, having perforated the fifth intercostal space (space between the ribs) and deeply beyond it.[27] "If the blow with the lance had been given from the left it would have pierced the ventricles, which in a corpse have no blood in them. There would have been no flow of blood but only water. . . ."[28]

The correlations between the scriptural account of the sufferings of Christ on the Cross with those depicted on the Shroud of Turin are too compelling to be considered merely coincidental.

## –4–

# The Sudarium of Oviedo

ONE cloth which can contribute a great deal to the study of the Shroud of Turin and its authenticity is the Sudarium of Oviedo. This cloth has been kept in Spain since the seventh century and housed in the cathedral of Oviedo, a town in the north of Spain, since the eleventh century. The *sudarium* is a piece of bloodstained cloth woven with the same type of thread as the Shroud. The cloth bears no image and measures two feet nine inches by one foot nine inches. It is believed by many to be the face cloth or napkin that covered the face of Christ when He was taken down from the Cross. The *sudarium* is mentioned in the Gospel of St. John: "Then Simon Peter came, following him, and went into the tomb; he saw the linen cloths lying, and the napkin, which had been on his head, not lying with the linen cloths but rolled up in a place by itself" (*John* 20:6-7). According to Jewish burial traditions, it was considered impertinent to show the disfigured face of a dead man. Therefore, a sweat cloth or a napkin was placed over the face and was then discarded at the tomb.

The history of the *sudarium* is better documented than that of the Shroud of Turin. Much of our information on the cloth comes from the writings of Bishop Pelayo, who was bishop of Oviedo in the twelfth century. According to his *Book of the Testaments of Oviedo* and the *Chronicon Regum Legionensium*, the *sudarium* was preserved in Jerusalem up to the year 614, when the city was conquered by the Persian King Chosroes II, who reigned from 590 to 628.[1] At that time a priest by the name of Filipo took the cloth and other relics, which were kept in a cedar chest to Alexandria for safekeeping. When Chosroes conquered Alexandria in 616, the cloth was taken across the north of Africa to evade the advancing Persians. The cloth was then brought to Spain via Cartagena where Saint Fulgentius, bishop of Ecija, received the chest, or holy ark, along with the fleeing refugees. In turn, he entrusted the holy ark containing the *sudarium* to Saint Leandro, Bishop of Seville. Leandro once lived in Constantinople from 579 to 582 and may very well have seen the Shroud itself. Evidence for this can be gleaned from a verse in the Mozarabic Liturgy for Easter Saturday which is associated with Leandro. In the *Illatio* we read: "Peter ran to the tomb with John and saw the recent imprints of the dead and risen one on the cloths."[2] This makes for another interesting connection between the Shroud and the *sudarium*.

Saint Isidore later succeeded Saint Leandro as Bishop of Seville. One of Isidore's disciples was Saint Braulio, Bishop of Zaragoza (585-651). In the eighteenth century, twenty-four of his letters were discovered in Lyons. In one of his letters written in 631 to a priest named Tayo, Braulio says:

> But at that time they knew about many things that happened but were not written down, as one reads concerning the linen cloths, and the *sudario* with which the Lord's body was enveloped, that it was found, but one does not read that it was preserved. For I do not believe that it was ignored, with the result that these relics were not kept by the Apostles for future times, and other things of that sort.[3]

Isidore was eventually succeeded by Saint Ildefonso, who had been his student. When Ildefonso was appointed Bishop of Toledo in 657, he took the chest with him where it remained until 718. With the invasion of the Moors at the beginning of the eighth century, the chest containing the *sudarium* was taken farther north to Asturias, according to some authors, to avoid destruction. It was here that it first became designated as the "holy ark." Initially it was kept in a cave now known as Monsacro, six miles from Oviedo. In 840, King Alfonso II commissioned a special chapel in the cathedral, called the *Camara Santa*, to house the holy ark.

The fact that the *sudarium* has been in the region of Asturias from ancient times cannot be disputed. On March 14, 1075, the holy ark was opened on the occasion of a visit by King Alfonso VI. Also present were his sister Urraca Fernandez and Rodrigo Diaz de Vivar, better known as El Cid. At this time a list was made of its contents. The King ordered that the chest be silver-plated to honor the precious relics. The bas relief includes images of Our Lord, the Twelve Apostles and the Four Evangelists. This work was finally realized in 1113. An inscription on the reliquary reads: "*el Santo Sudario de N.S.J.C.*" ("the Holy Sudarium of Our Lord Jesus Christ").

## Science and the Sudarium

Much of the scientific research on the *sudarium* has been carried out by the *Equipo de Investigacion del Centro Español de Sindonologia* (EDICES) under the direction of Guillermo Hermas and Dr. Jose Villalain of the University of Valencia. They first studied the *sudarium* in late 1989 and early 1990.

## Pollen on the Sudarium

During their studies they excised minute samples of the cloth and also tested pollen and dust from its surface. Previous research on the cloth had been carried out by Monsignor Giulio Ricci and Dr. Max Frei, who took pollen samples from the Shroud of Turin. Frei conducted similar pollen tests on the *sudarium* and found pollen from Jerusalem, Oviedo, Toledo and North Africa, consonant with the ancient account of the *sudarium's* itinerary.[4] Of the thirteen pollens that were found, eight were on both the Shroud and the *sudarium*.[5] There is no evidence on the cloth of any pollen which is indigenous to Turkey, Constantinople, France or Italy, which are believed to be the locations along the route the Shroud traveled. Subsequent pollen studies conducted by Dr. Carmen Gomez Ferreras, a biologist at the University of Complutense in Madrid, found pollen from three genera of plants identified as *quercus*, *pistacia* and *tamarix*, which are native to the region of Palestine.[6]

## Stain Marks

Perhaps the most obvious characteristics of the *sudarium* are its numerous stain marks. Scientific analysis has shown that the main stains are composed of one part blood and six parts of pulmonary oedema fluid.[8] It has also been established that when a person dies by crucifixion, "his lungs are filled with the fluid from the oedema. If the body is moved or jolted, this fluid can come out through the nostrils."[9] This finding is consistent with the manner in which the man on the Shroud died.

## POLLEN TRACES FOUND ON SUDARIUM OF OVIEDO

(Based on chart by Carmen Gomez Ferreras)[7]

| Name of Pollen | Number |
|---|---|
| ANACARDIACEAE | |
| *T. Pistacia terebinthus* | 1 |
| BETULACEAE | |
| *Alnus glutinosa* | 7 |
| *Corylus avellana* | 3 |
| CARYOPHYLLACEAE | |
| *T. Paronychia capitata* | 1 |
| CHENOPODIACEAE | |
| *T. Chenopodium album* | 7 |
| COMPOSITAE | |
| *T. Artemisia campestris* | 2 |
| *T. Senecio vulgaris* | 1 |
| CRUCIFERAE | |
| *T. Raphanus raphanistrum* | 1 |
| CUPRESSACEAE | |
| *T. Juniperus oxycedrus* | 4 |
| FAGACEAE | |
| *Castanea sativa* | 3 |
| *T. Quercus perennifolius* | 5 |
| GRAMINEAE | |
| *T. Graninea silvestris* | 20 |
| LEGUMINOSEAE | |
| *T. Lotus creticus* | 18 |

| | |
|---|---|
| *T. Cytisus scoparius* | 13 |
| *T. Trifolium repens* | 7 |
| LILIACEAE | |
| *T. Allium roseum* | 2 |
| OLEACEAE | |
| *Olea europaea* | 1 |
| PLANTAGINACEAE | |
| *T. Plantago coronopus* | 1 |
| PINACEAE | |
| *T. Pinus pinea* | 26 |
| ROSACEAE | |
| *T. Rubus ulmifolius* | 4 |
| SALICACEAE | |
| *T. Salix triandra* | 1 |
| *T. Populus alba* | 3 |
| TAMARICACEAE | |
| *T. Tamarix africana* | 4 |
| UMBELLIFERAE | |
| *T. Daucus carota* | 2 |
| URTICACEAE | |
| *T. Parietaria* | 4 |
| TOTAL NUMBER OF POLLENS | 141 |

The remarkable aspect about the bloodstains on the *sudarium* is that they match exactly the shape and form of the face of the man on the Shroud. Dr. Alan Whanger, professor emeritus of psychiatry at Duke University Medical Center in Durham, North Carolina, and his wife Mary, developed the polarized image overlay technique which, in order to make comparisons, allows for two images to be superimposed using polarized filters. When they applied this technique to the *sudarium* and the Shroud, they found over seventy-five congruent blood stains on the facial portion of the two cloths and fifty-five congruent blood stains on the back of the head and neck.[10]

Consequently, Dr. Whanger believes that these one hundred thirty points of congruence between the *sudarium* and the Shroud provide overwhelming evidence that both linens touched the same person. In a court of law, only forty-five to sixty points of congruence are needed to establish a facial identity. Professor Avinoam Danin, a botanist from Hebrew University in Jerusalem, and the world authority on the flora of the Near East, said: "There's no possibility that this cloth in Oviedo and the Shroud would both have the same blood stains and these pollen grains unless they were covering the same body."[11] Also noteworthy about the facial characteristics of the two cloths is that both exhibit typical Jewish features: a prominent nose measuring eight centimeters or a little over three inches, and high cheek bones. What is more, the beard of the *sudarium* matches that of the Shroud perfectly. There is also a high concentration of dust in the nasal area suggesting that the man may have fallen on his face.

According to the Spanish Investigation Team, EDICES, the *sudarium* must have been in contact with the dead man's face for a short duration of time because it was stained by fresh blood, not coagulated blood. The cloth was folded over, albeit not in the middle, and the blood soaked through the cloth. This accounts for the four-fold identical stains.

The time interval between the body being taken down from the cross and carried to the tomb is crucial to understanding the stain formation. Over six thousand experimental stains were made using a reconstructed model of a head with tubes in the nostrils from which liquid could exude. From these experiments Dr. Villalain has been able to calculate that the head of the man on the cross was tilted seventy degrees forward and twenty degrees to the right.[12] The *sudarium* was wrapped only around the left side of the man's head because his right cheek was almost on his right shoulder. Dr. Whanger is of the opinion that the crown of thorns may still have been on the head because there are numerous hole marks on the *sudarium* which may have been caused by thorns. Dr. Villalain was also able to discern finger marks rather than the fingerprints of the person who held the cloth to the man's face: "The first time that pressure was applied to the cloth over the dead man's face was by a left hand, with the index, middle, ring and little fingers bent inwards, resting on the palm of the hand, and the thumb resting on the knuckle of the index finger."[13] By thus positioning the hand, the individual was able to push the nose of the deceased upwards with the palm of the hand to curb the blood flow. At this time the first set of stains was made. Tests conducted by the Spanish Investigation Team indicate that the body remained on the cross for approximately one hour before being taken down: "This time the hand and arm came from the other direction, i.e. over the head, which means that the person was behind the head of the dead body. The thumb was pressed to the right hand side of the corpse's nose, and the index finger to its left hand side. The other three fingers were bent, resting on the cloth over the body's cheek."[14]

When the body was removed from the cross, it would have been laid face-down for about forty-five minutes, during which time blood and other fluids would have come out of the nostrils. Then the second set of stains would have been made. The last set of stains was likely made when the body was lifted from the ground where it was lying at the foot of the cross: "the left hand was in a very similar position to the previous one. The only difference was that both the index and middle fingers were applying pressure to the left-hand side of the man's nose, in another attempt to stem the abundant blood flow. During this whole process, the position of the sudarium over the face did not change."[15] It was this last position of the hand over the face which made it possible to obtain the measurement of eight centimeters for the length of the nose.

Blood samples from the *sudarium* analyzed by Dr. Pierluigi Baima Bollone, a medical examiner from the University of Turin, and the Roman hematologist, Dr. Carlo Goldoni, have verified that the blood is human blood of the type AB. This is the same blood type found on the Shroud of Turin. Blood type of this group is common in the Middle East but rare in Europe, which is another convincing argument that the possibility is remote of the Shroud and/or the *sudarium* having been fabricated in Europe. Also intriguing is that this blood type matches that of the Eucharistic miracle of Lanciano, Italy.

Briefly, in Lanciano there is reserved in an ornate reliquary one of the oldest Eucharistic miracles in the history of the Catholic Church. Around the year 700 A.D., a Basilian priest who doubted the Real Presence of Jesus Christ in the Eucharist celebrated Mass one day in the Church of Saints Legontian and Domitian. During the words of Consecration, the Host turned to visible flesh, and the wine became visible blood. The Blood separated into five unequal pellets, all of which when weighed together weighed as much as each one separately. Scientific studies conducted in 1971 by Professor Odoardo Linoli from the University of Siena determined the blood type to be AB.[16]

## Aloes and Myrrh

In his Gospel, St. John the Evangelist writes, "Nicodemus . . . came bringing a mixture of myrrh and aloes which weighed about a hundred pounds. They took Jesus' body, and in accordance with Jewish burial custom bound it up in wrappings of cloth with perfumed oils" (*John* 19:39-40). In one of his books on the Shroud, Monsignor Ricci references a statement made by the custodian of the *sudarium*, who reassured him that a chemical examination of the cloth found the presence of aloes and myrrh.[17] However, subsequent research by Felipe Montero Ortego, from Madrid, an expert who used electronic microscopes, did not confirm their presence, but found residues of monosacharides which are similar to aloes and myrrh.[18]

## –5–

# Scientific Studies: 1898-1973

THE first scientist to conduct a scientific inquiry of the Shroud was a Frenchman by the name of Paul Vignon of the *Institute Catholique*. He was born into a wealthy family in Lyons in 1865 and was a biologist as well as an artist.

In early 1900, after hearing of the mysterious photographs taken of the Shroud by Secondo Pia in 1898, he met with Pia and was convinced that the image on the Shroud could not have been painted. Vignon worked closely with Yves Delage, a professor of anatomy at the Sorbonne. Their association was unique in that Vignon was a devout Catholic while Delage was an agnostic. Delage concurred that the photographs of the Shroud were anatomically correct and could not have been produced by an artist.

Vignon conducted a series of experiments to ascertain how the image came to be imprinted on the cloth. He obtained pieces of old linen with a weave and thickness resembling that of the Shroud. He then painted them with oils and watercolors and allowed them to dry. When they were dried, he rolled them up and noticed, as would be expected, that the paint cracked and peeled off. This was enough evidence to convince Vignon that the Shroud image was not a painting. He then hypothesized that the image could have been made with a light dye that diffused into the fibrils of the linen cloth. If this were so, then the liquid would have spread along the threads leaving vein-like patterns, which is not the case on the Shroud. Furthermore, such dyes would not have been affected by the chemical changes that could produce a negative image.

Next, Vignon studied the wound marks on the Shroud and concluded: "We have only to look at the wound-marks to be able to say that they are not the work of a forger."[1] He based his conclusion on the shape of the wounds as well as how the blood clotted on the linen cloth: "The linen is actually stained the same colour as the clots by contact with them, and is therefore also darker at the edges and less dark in the middle. That is why these marks are positive."[2] Artists of the Middle Ages and prior to that time did not depict blood clots in a realistic manner.

Having dismissed the idea that the image on the Shroud was a forgery, Vignon became intent on discovering how the image had come to be transferred onto the cloth. Wearing a false beard, he covered his face and body with red chalk and lay down on an operating table. His colleagues then placed a linen cloth on him coated with albumen that acted as "lint tape" to which the chalk would adhere. The experiment failed to produce the vivid details of the Shroud. Naturally, the parts of the cloth not touched by the body did not pick up anything. Furthermore, the images that were picked up were distorted.[3]

Vignon was now even more intent on proving the Shroud's authenticity. He began to postulate that somehow the image was produced by vaporization. He and an associate, Rene Colson, studied Jewish burial customs. They found that a mixture of myrrh and aloes was often combined with olive oil to make an unguent which was applied to the body or the cloth or both. Aloe contains two chemical principles, namely, aloin and aloetine. When aloin is added to water it gives a yellow tone. Aloetine, on the other hand, which oxidizes quickly with alkalies, would turn brown.

Vignon and Colson knew that vaporized ammonia could produce images. Ammonia is the by-product of fermented urea which is largely excreted by the body in urine and in small amounts through perspiration. A body which has undergone severe torture can emit what is known as morbid sweat. Once fermented, urea becomes a carbonate of ammonia, and this would produce alkaline vapors that could stain the spices and olive oil on the Shroud.[4]

On April 21, 1902, before Vignon published his book, Delage presented their findings in a lecture at the Paris Academy of Sciences. In his paper, "The Image of Christ Visible on the Holy Shroud of Turin," Delage explained how the wounds and other evidence were anatomically correct, which excluded the possibility of the Shroud being forged. His presentation caused such a controversy that the secretary of the Academy refused to print in the Academy's journal, *Comptes rendus*, any section of Delage's paper that indicated the image on the Shroud was that of Jesus Christ.

Delage was so taken aback at how his presentation was received that he soon abandoned all interest in the topic of the Shroud and pursued other areas of study. He expressed his feelings of dismay in a letter to the editor of *Revue Scientifique*:

> When I paid you a visit in your laboratory several months ago to introduce you to Vignon . . . had you the presentiment of the impassioned quarrels which this question would arouse . . .?
>
> I willingly recognize that none of these given arguments offer the features of an irrefutable demon-

> stration, but it must be recognized that their whole constitutes a bundle of imposing probabilities, some of which are very near being proven . . . a religious question has been needlessly injected into a problem which in itself is purely scientific, with the result that feelings have run high, and reason has been led astray. If, instead of Christ, there were a question of some person like a Sargon, an Achilles or one of the Pharaohs, no one would have thought of making any objection. . . . I have been faithful to the true spirit of science in treating this question, intent only on the truth, not concerned in the least whether it would affect the interests of any religious party. . . . I recognize Christ as a historical personage and I see no reason why anyone should be scandalized that there still exist material traces of his earthly life.[5]

In contrast, Vignon remained undaunted and continued his study of the Shroud. Although he could never duplicate his vaporograph process exactly in the laboratory, it became the leading theory of image formation for years to come.

One of the most comprehensive anatomical studies of the Shroud was conducted by Dr. Pierre Barbet, who saw the Shroud in 1933. Barbet was the surgeon general of St. Joseph Hospital in Paris. Working mainly from Enrie's photographs, he conducted a number of tests using volunteers, amputated limbs and cadavers. Barbet's studies support the conclusion that the man on the Shroud had all the signs of a victim who had been tortured and crucified.

Similar research was conducted in the 1950s by Dr. Hermann Moedder, a German radiologist at St. Francis Hospital in Cologne. He engaged university students to volunteer having their arms suspended from crosses. In this way he was able to determine the physical effects of crucifixion. He was followed by an English physician, David Willis, in the 1960s, who compiled all medical studies of the Shroud available at that time.

## Secret Commission of 1969

In 1969, Michele Cardinal Pellegrino of Turin appointed a commission to examine the Shroud. Among the group were Monsignor Pietro Caramello, chairman; Monsignor Jose Cottino, vice-chairman; Monsignor Sergio Baldi, secretary; Professor Silvio Curto, curator of the Egyptian Museum of Turin; Professor Enzo DeLorenzi, head of the radiology department at Mauriziano Hospital in Turin; Professor Giorgio Frache, from the Institute of Forensic Medicine at the University of Modena; Dr. Noemi Gabrielli, retired director of the art galleries of Piemonte; Dr. Giovanni Battista Judica Cordiglia, photographer and lecturer in Forensic Medicine at the University of Milan; and Professors Camillo Lenti, Enrico Medi and Luigi Gedda. Because this effort was not widely known by the general public, it is often referred to as "the secret commission."

On June 16-17, 1969, the commission examined the Shroud and concluded that it was in good condition. It also offered precautionary measures that needed to be taken to preserve the Shroud from deterioration and suggested proposals for further scientific research.

Sample threads from the Shroud were taken which showed that the linen fabric was mixed with cotton. This was an interesting discovery, given that cotton does not grow in Europe. The cotton in the cloth corresponds to a Middle Eastern variety known as *G. herbaceum*. According to the Mosaic law, there was a prohibition against combining linen and wool (cf. *Lev.* 19:19; *Deut.* 22:11). However, it was licit to combine cotton and wool. That being the case, it would not have been considered unlawful for a weaver to use the same loom to weave cotton and linen.

## Studies of 1973

On November 23, 1973, permission was granted by Cardinal Pellegrino and the then owner of the Shroud, exiled King Umberto II of Savoy, to have a televised exposition of the Shroud. Following the telecast, new studies of the Shroud ensued. At this time the scientists were allowed to remove sample threads from the Shroud for analysis. A total of seventeen threads were extracted. Among the participants were Dr. Cesare Codegone, director of the department of technological physics at the Polytechnic of Turin; Professor Curto; Professor Gabrielli, Professor DeLorenzi, Dr. Frache and his colleagues, Dr. Eugenia Mari Rizzati and Dr. Emilio Mari; Professor Guido Filogamo from the Institute of Human Anatomy at the University of Turin; and his colleague, Alberto Zina. Also invited were Dr. Cordiglia; Professor Mario Milone, director of the Institute of Chemistry at the University of Turin; Dr. Max Frei, a Swiss criminologist and botanist; and Professor Gilbert Raes, a Belgian textile expert from the Ghent Institute of Textile Technology.

Their individual findings were published in January 1976. Some of their results include the following:

- Dr. Codegone published a dissertation on the inadvisability of performing a carbon-14 dating test on the Shroud, because such a test would not be reliable.
- Professor DeLorenzi did not believe that radiological

tests would produce any meaningful results:

> Radiographs of works of art, especially canvas paintings (as they are objects very similar to the relic of the Holy Shroud), provide interesting results because of the use of pigments made from heavy metals (lead, zinc, mercury, etc.). This situation does not exist for the Holy Shroud, and only if other research projects give grounds for suspecting the existence of heavier elements in a high-enough concentration, could a radiological examination be recommended.[6]

- Doctors Frache, Mari and Rizzati examined five individual threads from the bloodstained areas of the Shroud but were not willing to concede that the stains were indeed blood. They did find that the body image appeared on the upper surface of the cloth and was composed of yellow fibrils that did not penetrate the linen: "These granulations affected the majority of the fibers, indeed substantially so, but they were not found in the spaces between the fibers."[7] They did not, however, check the dorsal side of the Shroud to see if the body image there was as superficial as that on the front.
- Professor Curto's study was on the nature of the cloth. While he did not exclude the possibility of its authenticity, he favored the theory that it was an artistic painting which made use of some kind of model:

> For our part, we must say that we are inclined to think that it is an artistic impression, and if we accept this supposition, we cannot say that the style of the figure is of the late-ancient period, because of the psychology expressed in the face and the perfect anatomical details: consequently, due to the fact that the transfixion of the wrists could only

> have resulted from observations made during the 13th century or later, it could have been produced almost at any time after that.[8]

- Professors Filogamo and Zino made microscopic examinations of two threads to determine whether or not blood was present: "The Shroud threads were seen to be composed of numerous plant fibers. Both threads showed, on the surface of several fibers, the characteristic presence of granules having different forms and diameter, and of a red colour."[9] Their test results were inconclusive.
- Professor Gabrielli stated that although there was no evidence of pigment or dye in the image areas, the image was the product of an artist's painting or stamping:

> There is no evidence from tests under the microscope that it could be a painting, which would have required previous treatment of the cloth with a special preparation containing non-absorbent, insulating substances—a treatment called priming. . . . Therefore . . . [I] suggest a second hypothesis, which I consider more likely. That is, that the artist's effort was not engraved on a wooden block, as required by the printing process, but was drawn by the artist directly onto a wet cloth stretched on a frame, using a compound of sepia-coloured clay and yellow ochre diluted in a resinous liquid, and that this original, while still wet, was then spread out over the Shroud, also well stretched, and pressed against it with a padded weight, as it used to be done for printing.[10]

- Professor Raes found minute fibers of cotton mixed in with the linen. He also noticed that it was spun in a "Z" twist pattern and woven in a three-to-one twill, meaning that the horizontal (weft) thread passes alternately over three and under one of the vertical (warp) threads. The number of threads in each square centimeter is approximately twenty-four in the weft and thirty-six in the warp.

- Max Frei, who founded the Zurich Police Scientific Laboratory and was its director for twenty-five years, took twelve sticky tape samples from the surface of the Shroud and discovered pollen spores on them. During the next several months he analyzed and photographed them and claimed to have identified pollen from fifty-seven different plants.[11] While some of the pollen came from plants indigenous to Europe, thirty-three of the plants were unique to Palestine and the areas of Turkey and Istanbul.

Given that the group did not study the Shroud previously and did not collaborate with one another, it is not surprising that they were not able to come up with any conclusive results. Their work, however, opened the path for further scientific inquiry, as we shall see in succeeding chapters.

## –6–

# The 1978 STURP Study

THE year 1978 marked the 400th anniversary of the Shroud's transfer from Chambery to Turin. To celebrate this occasion, the newly-appointed Archbishop of Turin, Anastasio Ballestrero, through the diplomatic efforts of Fr. Peter Rinaldi, a Salesian priest stationed in New York, had the Shroud exposed for public veneration from August 27–October 8. Following this exposition, over forty scientists from Italy and America were given five days to carry out non-destructive tests on the Shroud. The thirty-plus members of the American group known as the "Shroud of Turin Research Project," or STURP, were headed by Dr. John Jackson and Dr. Eric Jumper, two United States Air Force captains and physicists. The team brought with them seventy-two crates of equipment. The group was composed of specialists from different disciplines: Donald Lynn headed a group from the Jet Propulsion Laboratory of Pasadena, including Jean Lorre, and Donald Devan from the Oceanographic Services, Inc., of Santa Barbara. Bill Mottern, from the Sandia Laboratories, led the team of specialists who carried out a series of radiography exams of the Shroud with the following group from Los Alamos National Scientific Laboratories: Robert Dinegar, Donald and Joan Janney, Larry Schwalbe, Diane Soran, Ron London, Roger Morris, and Ray Rogers who took various sticky tape samples of dust particles from the surface of the Shroud. Joseph Accetta from Lockheed

Corporation coordinated the group that inspected the Shroud with infrared rays. Roger and Marion Gilbert from the Oriel Corporation of Connecticut examined the light spectrum emitted by fluorescence beneath ultraviolet lighting.

Also participating in the examination of the Shroud were Steven Baumgard and John German from the U.S. Air Force Weapons Laboratories; Robert Bucklin, medical examiner; Joseph Gambescia, chairman of medicine at St. Agnes Medical Center in Philadelphia; Rudolph Dichtl from the University of Colorado; Ken Stevenson from IBM; Thomas D'Muhala from the Nuclear Technology Corporation; and Thomas Haverty from Rocky Mountain Thermograph. Photographers included the following: Ernest Brooks, Vernon Miller and Mark Evans from the Brooks Institute of Photography in Santa Barbara, CA; Barrie Schwortz; and Sam Pellicori, an optical physicist from the Santa Barbara Research Center. Dr. Max Frei, the Swiss botanist and criminologist who had taken pollen samples back in 1973, attended as well.

In addition, a small group of Sisters of St. Joseph was present. The Sisters' services were utilized to unstitch a portion of the protective cloth which had been added to the Shroud in 1534 so that a mini-vacuum could extract some dust particles. Sample threads were also taken from different areas of the Shroud.

Availing themselves of the 120 hours given to them during the five days allotted, the scientists worked on the Shroud around the clock. They conducted extensive tests, taking some 30,000 photographs. These tests included X-ray fluorescence spectrometry; macro/micro(scopic) observations; photomacrographs; sticky tape samples; low energy X-radiography; photo-electric and photographic fluorescence; infra-red, visible and ultra-violet reflectance spectra; photographic images of wavelength regions, including thermal emission images; and electron microscopy and microprobe. In addition to these tests, other independent tests were done later in the United States, yielding various findings, including the following:

- One of the first tests conducted measured the thickness of the cloth in order to determine heat penetration (one of the theories was that the image was formed by scorching). The cloth measured approximately 345 microns thick (about one hundredth of an inch). If the image were heat-induced, the heat-emitting object would have had to be on the cloth for less than one second in order for the image to be so light. The body image on the Shroud is only on the uppermost fibers of the cloth. It is highly improbable that such a large image was produced by a hot object in a split second.

  For purposes of clarification, the terms "fiber," "fibril" and "thread" will be defined. A thread is composed of one hundred or more fibers. Each thread is about one-seventh of a millimeter wide. When fiber is separated, it is called a fibril; each fibril is fifteen microns in diameter.
- The coloration goes only one to two fibers deep into the thread structure. If the image were painted on the cloth, the paint would have penetrated the fibers. As it is, the fibers are not stuck to one another as would be expected if pigment had been used.
- Under microscopic examination it was discovered that the image is monochromatic, meaning that the yellow discoloration of the fibers is the same throughout the image. The darker areas are not *more* yellow; instead, the variations in color scheme are due to the *number* of fibers that are discolored.

- In transmitted light (i.e., light directed from behind the cloth), the image "disappears," while the scorch marks from the fire of 1532 have a faint reddish-brown hue. This means that the body image does not penetrate the fibrils like the fire scorch marks.
- Thirty-two sticky tape samples were taken from various areas of the Shroud, including image areas. The tape pulled away more easily from the image areas than from the non-image areas of the cloth. Upon examination of these samples under a microscope, it was revealed that there were more yellow fibrils from image areas than from non-image areas. Some of the particles which were observed on the tapes included pollen, wool, parts of insects, dog hairs, wax, red silk, blue linen, glass, pink spantex and several kinds of red and black particles. The various colored particles on the Shroud could be residue from painted religious articles placed by devotees on the cloth to keep as a relic. As for the red silk, we know that, up to the exhibition in 1998, when the Shroud was not on display it was rolled up in a red covering provided by Princess Clotilde in 1868.
- There was no significant evidence of paint even though there were minute particles of iron oxide.
- The cloth covered a real human body.
- There were no signs of decomposition, indicating that the body had lain in a tomb for a short time or that the Shroud remained on the body for a short time.
- The blood stains on the cloth were real blood. The scientists who conducted this study were Dr. John Heller from the New England Institute and Dr. Alan Adler from Western Connecticut State University. Using a test known as microspectrophotometry, they discovered serum, blood proteins, hemoglobin, blood clots, porphyrin and bilirubin. Although Heller and

Adler did not test for blood type, the Italian scientists determined that the blood was AB.[1]

The following is a table of tests performed by Heller and Adler which confirmed the presence of whole blood on the Shroud:[2]

1. High iron in blood areas by X-ray fluorescence
2. Indicative reflection spectra
3. Indicative microspectrophotometric transmission spectra
4. Chemical generation of characteristic porphyrin fluorescence
5. Positive hemochromagen tests
6. Positive cyanmethemoglobin tests
7. Positive detection of bile pigments
8. Positive demonstration of protein
9. Positive indication of albumin specifically
10. Protease tests, leaving no residues
11. Microscopic appearance as compared with appropriate controls
12. Forensic judgment of the appearance of the various wound and blood marks.

The high presence of iron on the Shroud is significant, as iron is a major component of blood. Also noteworthy is the presence of bile residue known as bilirubin. This occurs when blood begins to break down, particularly after someone has suffered a severe trauma. "Bilirubin is . . . the stuff that makes jaundice."[3] It only takes three out of the twelve blood tests to prove the presence of whole blood in a court of law. On the Shroud there are four times that number.

- Scientists discovered a correlation between image intensity and the distance from the cloth to the skin (approximately 3.7 cm). That is, the closer the body is to the cloth, the darker the body image. This gives the man on the Shroud a three-dimensional appearance which would not occur if the image were a typical two-dimensional painting. John Jackson and Eric Jumper, along with Bill Mottern of Sandia Laboratory in Albuquerque first demonstrated this in 1976 using a VP-8 Image Analyzer with black and white photos of the Shroud taken by Enrie in 1931. For Jackson, this is a "confirmation that the Shroud covered a body shape at the time of image formation."[4]

- Around a number of bloodstains can be seen halo-like stains which most likely are serum. These stains are clearly seen under ultraviolet fluorescence.[5]
- The left knee shows bad lacerations and contusions, likely caused by falling: "There was dirt on the sole of the foot, and minute abrasions with blood and some dirt on the tip of the nose and on one knee. It was as though the man had fallen, unable to break the fall with his hands, and partly skinned his knee and nose."[6] Minute dirt particles from the foot were analyzed by Joseph Kohlbek at the Hercules Aerospace Laboratory in Salt Lake City, Utah. He determined the particles to be travertine aragonite, which is a rare kind of calcite found in Jerusalem. This finding was later confirmed by Dr. Ricardo Levi Setti from the Enrico Fermi Laboratory at the University of Chicago.[7]
- The Shroud image is thermally and chemically stable, meaning that the color of the image was not affected either by the fire of 1532 nor the water used to extinguish the fire. If an artist had used inorganic pigments, the image would have been altered.
- There was no evidence of brush marks on the Shroud. The image on the cloth is composed of randomly

oriented markings. This was first brought to light by Jean Lorre and Donald Lynn in 1977.
- The image is caused by an alteration of the microfibrils of the cellulose structure of the cloth caused by oxidation, dehydration and conjugation of long-chain sugar molecules that make up the microfibrils. In other words, the very chemical makeup of the cloth fiber was changed in order to form the image.

Upon completion of their data collecting, the researchers spent another 250,000 hours analyzing their findings. Unfortunately, most of the data collected by STURP were published in professional journals and are not easily accessible to the general public. The main findings of the 1978 study are: the image is not formed by paint, there is evidence of human blood on the cloth, and the image formation must be caused by some cellulose oxidation/dehydration process. Ray Rogers declared: "I am forced to conclude that the image was formed by a burst of radiant energy—light if you like."[8]

# –7–

# The Case Against Authenticity

A LEADING skeptic of the Shroud's authenticity is Dr. Walter McCrone, a microanalyst from Chicago. McCrone gained international notoriety in 1974 for his study of the Vinland Map kept at Yale University. Briefly, the map was said to have been drawn by a monk from the Upper Rhine in the fifteenth century. The map indicated that it pre-dated Columbus' voyage. McCrone tested twenty-nine microparticles from the document and concluded that while the parchment was from the Middle Ages, the map was fraudulent because the ink consisted of anatase (titanium oxide, a synthetic pigment) which was not developed until the early twentieth century. In 1987, his conclusion was challenged by a group of scientists led by Dr. Thomas Cahill at the Crocker Nuclear Laboratory at the University of California at Davis. Employing a non-destructive technique called PIXE (particle induced X-ray emission), Cahill concluded that the ink of the Vinland Map contains only slight traces of titanium, which can be found in other genuine medieval documents. In fact, an authentic Gutenberg Bible (15th century) actually showed greater amounts of titanium than the Vinland Map. At a symposium held at Yale University Press on February 10, 1996 which was devoted to a discussion of the expanded version of the original book on the map, *The Vinland Map and the Tartar Relation*, Dr. Cahill said: "There is nothing about the chemistry or morphology of the Vinland Map that in any way makes it stand out from any of the parchments of that period that we have analyzed."[1] Dr. Wilcomb E. Washburn, the Director of American Studies at the Smithsonian Institution in Washington, who wrote the introduction to the new book, concurred: "I think the evidence is clearly on the side of authenticity."[2]

## Evidence of Paint?

Although Dr. McCrone was not part of the STURP team that examined the Shroud in Italy, Ray Rogers, the chemist from Los Alamos, provided McCrone with thirty-two sticky tape samples that he had taken from the surface of the Shroud during its examination in 1978. McCrone began to study the tape samples on Christmas Day 1978. He discovered a small quantity (not more than 10 milligrams) of iron oxide. The mixture was a combination of red and yellow pigment particles. Since this was found only on the blood areas of the Shroud, McCrone concluded that it was red pigment used by an artist. He postulated that the discoloration of the fibers could have been caused by the aging of that paint medium.[3] He then demonstrated how the paint could have been applied to the cloth without leaving any traces of brush strokes. Dipping his finger in powdered jeweler's rouge, he applied it to a piece of paper until there was little left on his finger; then he transferred that to a piece of linen.[4]

The STURP team did not accept McCrone's conclusions, because he did not take their findings into consideration, for example, that iron oxide is basically rust, which can be found in many forms of dust. Dr. Jackson made note that it was not surprising to find iron oxide in the blood areas of the Shroud because iron is a component of blood. Furthermore, the particles could have spread to other areas of the Shroud by the repeated folding and unfolding of the cloth throughout the centuries.

Another test conducted by McCrone was the amido black test.[5] This is a reagent that stains protein-based media. While the amido black test proved positive for the blood-mark areas, it was inconclusive in demonstrating that a protein medium, such as tempera, was used for the body image. Other scientists caution that the amido black test is unreliable because it can also stain cellulose, thereby giving a false reading.

In 1981, STURP held a meeting at Connecticut College in New London. McCrone, who had resigned from STURP in 1980, was invited to attend, but declined to participate. He later remarked: "I believe the shroud is a fake, but I cannot prove it."[6] During the presentation, Dr. Adler was asked to comment on McCrone's claim that there was no blood on the Shroud. Adler referred to a chart of the blood tests that he and Dr. Heller had performed and remarked: "That means that the red stuff on the Shroud is emphatically, and without any reservation, nothing else but B-L-O-O-D!"[7] McCrone's theory was dismissed by the use of X-ray fluorescence and visible light examination of the Shroud as well as microchemical tests. These studies showed that there was not a sufficient amount of iron oxide on the cloth to account for the least enhancement of the image.[8] The STURP team concluded that the iron oxide evidence was "irrelevant to the image formation process."[9]

## The Work of an Artist?

Two English researchers, Clive Prince and Lynn Picknett, have suggested that the Shroud image was painted by none other than Leonardo da Vinci. According to

Picknett, da Vinci created the image using an early photographic technique. Supposedly, a recently crucified body was used for the main image while Leonardo used a self-portrait for the face.[10] This hypothesis completely lacks credibility, for we know that there is documentary evidence that the Shroud was in Lirey in the 1350s and that it was given to the House of Savoy on March 22, 1453. Leonardo da Vinci was born in 1452. Isabel Piczek, an artist and physicist, said that

> most of Leonardo's paintings are . . . lost today because of his technical errors, despite the fact that he was one of the greatest masters of all time. So could he have created the Turin Shroud? It is not very likely. First, we would expect to find hundreds of sketches in his notebooks, describing the project from every angle and giving long instructions. We would also expect to find meticulously written records of the cost of the linen and all other materials used. He never once missed such information. . . . The image shows a cadaver in the state of rigor mortis. He would have had to finish his work before that condition changed, and that is a very limited time, too fast for the slow Leonardo. . . . Working at Leonardo's speed the man of the Shroud would have been not much more than a skeleton.[11]

With regard to the possibility of the image being painted, Piczek continued:

> Mediums cannot be thinned to the extent where they are rendered invisible because that renders the image invisible and incoherent. There is a coherent and continuous image on the Shroud. That fact—more than any other argument—excludes with superb precision the dependence of the image on any pigment

> particles which are not suspended in a continuous medium film of even marginal binding power.[12]

Scientists from STURP have concluded with certainty that there is no evidence that the Shroud image is a painting. Not only were no pigment particles found on the cloth, there was no evidence of brush strokes at all. Had the image been painted, the paint would have saturated through the cloth. On the contrary, the image is on the uppermost part of the fibrils. If one were to lift the brown fibrils, one would see white fibrils. According to Dr. Adler, "for a painter to have created this image, he would have needed a paintbrush the size of a fiber, which is less than half the width of a human hair."[13] He also remarked, "There was not enough iron oxide or vermilion to account for one painted drop of blood, let alone all the gore on the Shroud."[14] The "gore" to which he refers is the evidence of the man on the Shroud being tortured before He was crucified. Anatomical studies by Dr. Barbet in the 1930s, and others after him, show that the wounds are correct to the minutest detail. Such information would not have been known, or at least not portrayed with exactness, by an artist in the Middle Ages: "Medicine was primitive in the Middle Ages, still based on the concepts of the Roman anatomist, Galen, who practiced from 164 to 199 A.D. Medical illustrations from the 13$^{th}$-14$^{th}$ centuries exhibit these same primitive notions."[15] The image on the Shroud reveals that the blood image went on the cloth before the body image, for there was no yellow fiber image under the blood. If the image were forged by an artist, how could he apply the blood image first, then go back to put on the body image, and finally have the wounds and blood patterns match?

Another characteristic of the Shroud which precludes

it from being a painting is the element of foreshadowing. Piczek defines foreshadowing as "the placing of a human body into the geometrical system of perspective which will visually shorten its parts, yet retain the illusion of proper proportion."[16] An untrained eye will look at the Shroud and conclude that the body lay flat on the cloth. This is not so. The body is actually bending forward, the head is bowing forward, and the knees are drawn up at least eight inches away from the cloth. As Piczek points out, "Since the Shroud image shows strong foreshadowing of the thighs, the lower legs and foreshortening of the torso, this absolutely excludes the fact that it could be a painting from the Middle Ages, when foreshortening was entirely unknown."[17]

Heller and Adler also conducted a battery of tests on the image fibers from the sticky tape samples. They tested for the presence of organic dyes and stains and discovered nothing. The chemists even tried to extract the yellow color with acids, bases and organic solvents, with no success. Attempts to bleach out the yellow were also unsuccessful.

## The Vapograph Theory

Paul Vignon first postulated the vapograph theory as a way to explain how the image of the man was transferred to the Shroud. Vignon did not advance his theory to prove forgery, but rather to argue that the image was caused by a natural means. The vapograph theory maintains that a chemical reaction between the ammonia in perspiration with the aloes, myrrh and olive oil on the Shroud caused the image.

Two members of the STURP team, Ray Rogers and Eric Jumper, tested this hypothesis and found serious flaws. First, vapors diffusing through space do not travel straight or in parallel lines. Secondly, the amount of morbid sweat on the body would not have produced sufficient ammonia to cause the image on the cloth. Even if it had, the gases would have permeated the cloth. On the contrary, the Shroud image is superficial.

According to Rogers, "I do not see how the image could be a reaction product of ammonia with aloes, because the organic product should be reasonably heat-sensitive."[18] He continues:

> Pure cellulose [a primary constituent of linen] begins to produce gaseous products at an appreciable rate shortly before 590 degrees Fahrenheit [310 degrees Centigrade]; unprocessed cotton batting and newsprint begin to pyrolyze [decompose] rapidly at about 446 degrees Fahrenheit [230 degrees Centigrade]. Parts of the Shroud were, then, subjected to temperatures sufficient to produce darkening for some unspecified time. Not all of the Shroud was darkened by the fire [of 1532]; therefore, a rather steep thermal gradient had to exist. However, parts of the image that are essentially in contact with darkened areas [caused by the fire] have, as nearly as can be observed, *identical* color tone and density as parts of the image at maximum distance from a discolored area. If large, complicated, natural-product organic molecules were responsible for the image, they should have decomposed, changed color or volatilized at different rates, depending on their distance from a high-temperature zone during the fire. There is no evidence for any variation at all.[19]

If the image had been formed by vapors, it would have been altered by the heat of the 1532 fire. This, however, is not the case.

Furthermore, a vapograph theory cannot account for the three-dimensional quality of the Shroud image. Rogers and Jumper concluded: "We view the evidence to be quite conclusive in ruling out the Vignon vapographic theory as an image formation hypothesis."[20]

## The Scorch Theory

Another theory that has been posited is that the image was somehow scorched onto the cloth. The scorch theory was first put forth in 1966 by Geoffrey Ashe, a British scholar. He was able to produce an image similar to the Shroud by exposing a piece of linen to radiant heat. Using a heated brass ornament of a horse, he discovered that placing a linen cloth over the heated object produced a clear negative image similar to the image on the Shroud. He concluded: "The Shroud is explicable if it once enwrapped a human body to which something extraordinary happened. It is not explicable otherwise."[21]

For the image to have been scorched onto the cloth the body would have had to produce mild heat, or light at moderate temperatures. According to Dr. Heller, "If it turns out that some form of molecular transport we have not been able to fathom is the method whereby the images of the scourged, crucified man were transferred to the linen, we shall have only solved another little micropart of the puzzle."[22]

One theory of how this energy transfer could have occurred was proposed by Giles Carter, a non-member of the STURP team. Carter, who is a professor of chemistry at Eastern Michigan University, theorized that X-rays emanating from the body caused the image on the Shroud. Studying photos taken by Vernon Miller, Carter "proposed that strong X-rays actually proceeded from within the bones and teeth of the dead man and then reacted with dust, dirt and chemicals on the skin, such as those caused by perspiration."[23] When questioned about Carter's work, Dr. Adler, who is known for his candor, remarked that the theory was "fine chemically, fine physically, yet bizarre biologically . . . the man would have been so radioactive that he glowed in the dark. Not to mention he would have been dead long ago from the radioactivity."[24]

Some have even postulated that a hot statue was used and placed onto the cloth to produce the image. Cellulose begins to yellow during the initial stages of burning. We know from the patches on the cloth that the Shroud did sustain some burn damage during the fire of 1532. If one were to observe the burn marks and the body image, one could conclude that they are identical. However, they are not. The fire scorches are redder than the body image. Under ultraviolet light the fire scorches fluoresce while the body image does not, and in transmitted light, the body image "disappears," while the scorch marks do not. Attempts to produce a heat-induced image only result in a distorted image and not a crisp image like that on the Shroud.

## The Latent-Image Theory

Sam Pellicori from Santa Barbara and John German from the U.S. Air Force Weapons Laboratories proposed that the image on the Shroud could have been caused by direct contact through a combination of body chemicals with heat or the linen cloth's natural aging process.

Pellicori tested this hypothesis in his laboratory by baking samples of linen at 150°C for seven and one-half hours. This technique caused the linen to yellow. He then applied myrrh, olive oil, and skin secretions to various parts of the linen and baked them for three and one-half hours. The results showed that the treated areas were more yellow than the non-treated area.

One of the problems with this theory is that there is not conclusive evidence for the presence of myrrh or olive oil on the Shroud. According to Ray Rogers: "Mass spectrometry . . . tested for aloes, myrrh, oils. . . . Everything came out negative."[25] Later research using immunofluorescence methods conducted in 1984 by Dr. Bollone and Agostino Gaglio found traces of aloes and myrrh on sample threads taken from the Shroud.[26]

Another problem with this Latent Image Theory is that it would require some pressure from the cloth to the body to account for the image formation. If that were so, then the frontal image of the Shroud would be lighter than the dorsal, for there would be more pressure applied to the back because the body lay directly on it. But the Shroud shows practically the same density on the front as well as the back of the image. Finally, the Latent Image Theory cannot account for the 3-D characteristic of the Shroud. As Dr. Heller explained: "The recessed areas of the face could not have been in contact with the cloth, as proved by the VP-8 images and the Shroud-body distance data. Pellicori agreed that that was still a problem for his hypothesis. It was not *a* problem, but rather *the* problem."[27]

## Powder-Rubbing Theories

In 1977 Joe Nickell, a professional "magician" (illusionist) who studied art at the University of Kentucky, tried to prove that the Shroud image was made very much in the manner that a brass rubbing is made from gravestones. After coating his face with a moist rouge, he attached canvas fabric loosely over a frame and made a print of his face. Subsequently, a photographer converted the negative into a positive image. Nickell first published his results in 1978. He admits that his initial experiment was "a failure—with distorted, overly wide eye sockets, a severely fractured bridge of the nose and a flattened nasal tip, among other flaws."[28] He then suggested that a wet cloth be applied to a bas-relief sculpture and allowed to dry, and then rouge be applied to it using a dauber. Dr. Jackson tried replicating Nickell's technique and said:

> We conformed, as Nickell indicates, wet linen to the bas-relief so as to make all image features (eyes, lips, etc.) impressed into the cloth. We then "dabbed" the cloth with fine tempera powder . . . the shaded image seemed to contain more curvature than distance information of the face; in addition, we noted large quantities of powder falling through the cloth weave structure and accumulating on the reverse side. Accordingly we conclude that this mechanism is unacceptable.[29]

A similar theory is espoused by two University of Tennessee professors, Emily Craig and Randall Breese. In 1994 they suggested that the image was produced using a powder pigment applied to a cloth which was placed face down on another cloth. The back side was then rubbed with the flat side of a wooden spoon or block of wood. Once the cloth was burnished, it was impervious to heat and water. The researchers refer to the work of Cennino Cennini, a medieval artist, to support their claim. However, Piczek argues that

> the success of the described method . . . depends on an initial drawing created with the use of carbon dust or iron oxide mixed with a binder and

> transferred from paper to canvas with a simple depression method and steam. This initial drawing, in order to have the qualities of the Shroud, would have had to introduce a degree of draftsmanship we cannot produce even today. . . .
>
> The authors refer to Cennino Cennini's handbook on art (1437) and to the writings of Theophilus (12th Century) as evidence for their technique being rooted in the Middle Ages. I have read and studied both of these. They do not even remotely reveal any dust transfer technique in art.[30]

The main flaw with the rubbing technique theory is that it cannot account for the 3-D quality of the image on the Shroud. What is more, there is no evidence of pigments or unguents on the cloth. According to Dr. Heller: "Adler and I found no traces of aloe, myrrh, or any other spice."[31] Finally, the use of bas-reliefs did not exist in medieval times. According to William Meacham, an archaeologist,

> Clearly, to be testable and viable, the hypothesis must derive from or at least not conflict with the known elements of 14th-century art. This it manifestly fails to do. . . . There is no rubbing from the entire medieval period that is even remotely comparable to the Shroud, nor is there any negative painting. Nickell's wet-mold-dry-daub technique was not known in medieval times according to art historian Husband and even that technique fails to reproduce the contour precision and three-dimensional effect, the lack of saturation points, and the resolution of the Shroud image.[32]

STURP scientists tested a number of different image formation theories and found them deficient. According to Heller, theories "such as hot statues, bas-reliefs, and so on . . . had long since been examined and rejected, because they could be ruled out—both theoretically and experimentally."[33]

It is the conclusion of STURP that none of the forgery or natural phenomenon theories can account for the image of the man on the Shroud. What is known is that, chemically speaking, the image is composed of dehydrated-oxidized cellulose of the cloth itself. How it was formed remains a mystery.

# –8–

# The Case For Authenticity

THE historical and scientific evidence related thus far provide incontrovertible data for the authenticity of the Shroud. In subsequent Shroud research, the following pathologists have made significant contributions: Dr. Bucklin, who was involved with STURP and is also deputy medical examiner for the county of Los Angeles; Dr. Frederick T. Zugibe, M.D., Ph.D., Chief Medical Examiner of Rockland County, New York; and Dr. Joseph Gambescia, a member of STURP and chairman of medicine at St. Agnes Medical Center in Philadelphia. Although they did not work together, these three doctors share a number of similar views. Doctors Bucklin and Gambescia usually concur with the arguments made by Dr. Barbet in the 1930s.

## Marks from the Wounds

Dr. Bucklin, who has been a forensic pathologist for over fifty years and has performed over 25,000 autopsies, has noted five major categories of wounds that can be identified on the Shroud.[1]

The first group of injuries is located on the back, ranging from the top of the shoulders down to the calf. These injuries consist of double puncture wounds which appear to go from lateral downward, indicating that an instrument was used in a flicking manner which tore the skin. In 1978, biblical archaeologist and scholar

Dr. Eugenia Nitowski, along with other scientists, discovered a minute muscle fragment on the man's back in an area designated 3BB.[2]

There are more than 120 strokes which were caused by a whip having either two or three dumbbell-shaped weights made of metal or bone. Based upon the wound patterns of the man on the Shroud, it appears that there were two tormentors, and that one of these scourgers was taller than the other and took particular interest in lashing the victim's legs. Dr. Zugibe envisions the scene as follows, based on his medical experience and Shroud research:

"Jesus was bent over and tied to a low pillar, when he was flogged across the back, chest, and legs with a multifaceted flagrum with bits of metal on the ends. Over and over again the metal tips dug deep into the flesh, ripping small vessels, nerves, muscles, and skin. . . . His mouth was dry, and his tongue stuck to the roof of his mouth. Unfortunately, the scourging was initiated by the Romans so that the Deuteronomic limit of forty lashes less one was not followed."[3]

The second group of injuries can be found on the face and head. The forehead and scalp have a series of bloodstains caused by sharp points. On the forehead one median flow and two lateral flows of blood are seen. Interestingly, the median stain is in the form of the number three on a negative photo, or the Greek letter *epsilon* on a positive photo, which, if turned on its side, forms the lower-case Greek letter *omega*. Recall the words of Christ: "I am the Alpha and the Omega" (*Rev*. 22:13).

## Wound on Hands

The third group of injuries involves the wrist and forearm. According to Dr. Barbet, a nail was most likely driven between the bones of the Space of Destot, the space between the bones of the wrist. When the nail entered this opening, it enlarged it without shattering any bones, but it injured the median nerve which flexes the thumbs, causing the thumbs to contract. Dr. Barbet pointed out: "That is why, on the shroud, the two hands when seen from behind only show four fingers, and why the two thumbs are hidden in the palms."[4]

These pioneer findings have been challenged by contemporary researchers like Dr. Zugibe, who says that the thumb naturally turns itself inward toward the index finger in both the living and the dead. He further states that the four bones which make up the Space of Destot, namely, the Capitate, the Semilunar, the Triquetral and the Hamate, are located on the ulnar (little finger) side of the wrist, not the radial (thumb) side, which is the side depicted on the Shroud.[5] Since the Shroud image only depicts the exit of the nail on the back of the hand, it is not certain at which point the nail entered. If the nail entered Destot's Space, it would not have severed the median nerve, because it is not located in this area. To support his hypothesis, Zugibe quotes from a book by Dr. Ernest Lampe, a renowned hand surgeon, who said that even if the median nerve was severed, "there is inability to flex the thumb, index and middle fingers."[6]

Zugibe suggests two possible places where the nail could have penetrated the hand: the radial side of the wrist, or at an angle through the thenar furrow located at the base of the thumb, that is, through the upper palm, slanted toward the wrist. He holds that the nail could very well have passed through the upper part of the palm, pointing toward the arm, emerging as shown on the Shroud. The upper part of the palm could easily have supported the weight of the body.

Another peculiar aspect of the man on the Shroud is that the left forearm looks shorter than the right. When one measures the tip of the elbow to the tip of the middle finger of each arm, the right forearm is three inches longer than the left.[7] In actuality, there is no difference. The optical illusion is due to the fact that the left wrist is bending forward over the right, and the fingers are curled.

## Wounds in the Feet

The fourth group of injuries is located around the feet. The imprint of the right foot is well defined. The left heel is elevated higher than the right, which may have retracted during rigor mortis. What is more, the fingerprints of the person who carried the body of Jesus to the tomb can be seen on the heels of the feet, most notably on that of the left foot. Monsignor Ricci observed: "The little finger, and the ring and middle fingers of the left hand, in contact with the heel, were surrounded by the blood running down from the hole in the left foot. The same thing happened with the right hand on the right heel, though the imprint is less clear."[8] When the image is viewed from the dorsal side, there is a complete imprint of the right foot that was likely pressed against the cross. This foot shows a bloodstain in the middle, whereas only the top heel of the left foot is visible over the right with a bloodstain visible on the outer portion. According to Dr. Bucklin:

> In examining the photograph of the right foot, we are able to make out an almost complete imprint. The border is slightly blurred in its middle part, but it still presents a very definite concavity

> corresponding to the plantar arch. More to the front the imprint is wider, and we can distinguish the imprint of five toes. The print is that which one might leave as he stepped on the flagstone with a wet foot.
>
> In this middle part of this footprint there is a small rectangular stain a little closer to the internal border than to the external border. This mark is quite definitely the mark of a nail and it can be seen that the nail has passed between the metatarsal bones at the base of the foot.[9]

Gambescia and Zugibe believe that two nails were used, whereas Jackson and Bucklin concur with Barbet that one nail was employed. Zugibe writes: "It is logical to assume that both feet were nailed separately and flush to the cross without being placed one on top of the other because to do this is easier to execute, no bones are broken, and it would correspond to the earliest Christian references."[10] Barbet's theory is that the nail entered through "one hole, piercing the two feet crossed one over the other, through the second intermetatarsal spaces, with the right foot against the cross and the left in front."[11] Dr. Jackson believes that the left foot was likely placed sideways over the right in such a way that the nail penetrated the heel of the top foot through the bottom without breaking any bones.

The one-nail theory is supported by a serendipitous find at a construction site in northern Jerusalem in June 1968. While workers were excavating for a building project in Giv'at ha'Mivtar, they discovered an ancient Jewish cemetery dating back to the Jewish revolt against Rome in 70 A.D. Archaeologists were called to examine the area, and they found over a dozen ossuaries, i.e., stone containers of bones.

Vasilius Tzaferis, an archaeologist, and Dr. Nicu Haas, a pathologist, studied the bones of one man identified as Jehohanan ben Ha'galgol, whose name was written in Aramaic on an ossuary.[12] They learned that he was a young man in his twenties, about five feet seven inches tall, who had a cleft-palate. The scientists also discovered holes in Jehohanan's wrist indicating that he was crucified. Of particular note was a nail fragment through the right heel bone. The nail was bent, probably because it hit a knot in the wood. According to Dr. Haas, the nail measured about seven inches and was driven through both the right and left heel bones. Wood splinters on the tip of the nail suggest that the vertical beam of the cross was olive wood, while the splinters on the head of the nail, which would have been at the heel bone, suggest that it was probably from a foot rest made of acacia wood.

At a conference given in Paris on November 27, 1988, Dr. Pierre Merat, an orthopedic surgeon, suggested that the nail wound of the man on the Shroud of Turin did not enter the metatarsal spaces, but rather, the tarsus. He states

> the passage of the nail to be between the second and the third cuneiform bone of the tarsus, above the scaphoid. . . . If a transparency of the skeleton [X-ray photo] is placed over the contour of the foot and these two transparencies are placed over the bloodstain of the cloth, the point where the nail emerges through the sole is evident. It is the little dark stain, surrounded by a clear halo, from which the blood ran down towards the ball of the foot.[13]

## The Asphyxiation Theory

A popular theory among researchers relative to the cause of death of the man on the Shroud is asphyxiation. This was first proposed back in 1925 by A. Lebec.[14] The reason for this hypothesis is associated with the two divergent streams of blood visible on the left wrist. It is believed that these distinct blood stains were caused by the crucified man lifting himself up on his feet in order to exhale. The weight on his arms would have caused his body to slump, compressing his lungs, thus making breathing difficult. To relieve pressure and to empty the lungs, the victim would have pushed up on his legs so that he could breathe. According to Barbet, the image on the Shroud shows that "the great pectoral muscles, which are the most powerful inspiratory muscles, have been forcibly contracted—they are enlarged, and drawn up towards the collar-bone and the arms."[15] At times, in order to hasten death, the executioner broke the legs of his victim with a *crucifragium* or mallet so that the crucified could not lift himself up. The man on the Shroud did not have his legs broken, which correlates with the scriptural account of Jesus' crucifixion in that His legs were not broken (*John* 19:33). This also fulfills the messianic prophecies: "He keeps all his bones; not one of them is broken" (*Ps.* 34:20 [33:21]) and "I can count all my bones." (*Ps.* 22:17 [21:18]).

The asphyxiation theory has since been challenged by Dr. Zugibe as untenable. He defines asphyxiation as "a physiological and chemical state which results from an inability of a living organism to obtain adequate oxygen for cell metabolism and to eliminate excess carbon dioxide. Usually, a six to ten minute span of complete respiratory obstruction causes irreversible brain damage and perhaps death."[16] We know that Jesus was on the

Cross for at least three hours (cf. *Matt.* 27:45; *Mark* 15:33; *Luke* 23:44). Zugibe is not convinced that the streams of blood visible on the left hand were caused by the man on the Shroud lifting himself up to exhale. One reason is that the bloodstains are located on the back of the hand, which was pressed against the cross. Secondly, if the man on the Shroud had lifted himself up repeatedly, the numerous blood vessels in the hand would have been severely damaged, causing a large blood stain all over the hand. "Another important point that militates against the two positions causing a 'double flow of blood' is the fact that the wrist does not change its angle even if the victim has to raise himself in order to breathe. The reason—*the arms bend at the elbows and not at the wrists*."[17]

Zugibe contends that a victim whose arms were outstretched upon a cross would not have difficulty breathing at an angle of 65 to 70 degrees. Even Barbet acknowledges that the image on the Shroud shows "the flow furthest from the hand . . . is at an angle of about 65° . . . the one nearest the hand . . . gives an angle of from 68° to 70°."[18] Zugibe suggests that given the pre-crucifixion torture that Jesus endured, as well as His agony on the cross, He most likely died of hypovolemic (low blood and fluid volume) shock. By definition, shock is "a state of inadequate perfusion of all cells and tissues, which at first leads to reversible hypoxic injury, but if sufficiently protracted or grave, to irreversible cell and organ injury and sometimes to the death of the patient."[19] If the shock was caused by low volume of blood and fluid, the cause of death would correspond to a traditional Christian belief regarding Christ's death, namely, that He died from loss of blood.

## Wound on the Side

The fifth group of injuries is the wound on the right side of the man on the Shroud, or our left (when looking at the negative image). The bloodstain here, partially hidden by a patch sewn on by the Poor Clares in 1532, measures 2¹/₄ inches wide and comes down about 6 inches. According to Barbet, "The greatest axis of this wound is just under 2 inches in length, while it has a height of about two-thirds of an inch . . . The inner end of the wound is 4 inches below and a little to the outside of the nipples, on a horizontal line running just under 4 inches below it."[20] The oval-shaped wound corresponds to the shape of a Roman lance which entered between the fifth and sixth ribs. As Barbet points out, "The blow of the lance which was given to the right side reached the right auricle of the heart, perforating the pericardium"[21] (the sac which surrounds the heart). If the lance had entered the left side of the chest, it would have penetrated the ventricles, which in a dead body do not contain blood. Bucklin likewise believes that this wound was inflicted after the man was dead, because the blood did not spurt out, but rather came out slowly.[22] He continues:

> The source of the blood cannot be seriously questioned, since it must have come from the heart. And from the position of the blood imprint, as well as its structures, it can be assumed that this blood came from the right side of the heart. This chamber was dilated after death, and when pierced by the lance, the blood readily flowed from it.[23]

In addition to the blood, a watery substance probably from the pleural cavity also flowed out and can be seen on the lower back of the image. This corresponds to the

Gospel account: "When they came to Jesus and saw that he was already dead, they did not break his legs. One of the soldiers thrust a lance into his side, and immediately blood and water flowed out" (*John* 19:33-34).

Bucklin attests: "If I were asked in a court of law to stake my professional reputation on the validity of the Shroud of Turin, I would answer very positively and firmly that it's the burial cloth of Christ—and that it is Jesus whose figure appears on the Shroud."[24]

## Blood on the Face

In 1986 Dr. Gilbert Lavoie began to ponder whether or not the blood on the hair of the man on the Shroud came out a bit too far on each side of the face. Using cutouts and tracings of a life-size picture of the Shroud face with the blood marks reproduced, Lavoie placed the cutout over his own face and discovered that the "blood" was not on the hair but on the forehead, temples and cheeks. This means that the bloodstains visible on the hair of the man on the Shroud were originally on his face. The importance of this discovery is that it sheds light on how the image was formed. Given that the body of the man on the Shroud was in a horizontal position, his hair would have fallen back naturally away from his face. But the image shows bloodstains on the hair on each side of the face, which means that the image formation did not occur when the cloth first made contact with the body. This strongly suggests that the image was formed when the man on the Shroud was in an upright (but not standing) position, with the cloth stretched. This could correspond to the moment of the Resurrection of Christ.

Lavoie makes three salient points regarding the blood on the face and hair:

1) The blood demonstrates a pattern that is consistent with that of a cloth having been draped over a supine body.
2) The direction of the blood flows illustrates that the body had previously been in a vertical position.
3) These blood marks are consistent in demonstrating that one process formed the blood marks and that another completely different process created the image.[25]

A corollary study of the facial bloodstains has been carried out by Professor Nicolo Cinquemani, a specialist in neurosurgery in Rome. Based on his study of Enrie's photographs, he suggests that Jesus moved His head downward by 10 cm (3.9 inches) during the Resurrection. This measurement was calculated by taking into account the length of the face determined to be 23.4 cm (9.1 in.), the height which equaled 187 cm, (6 ft. 1 in.) and the fact that the head is at a 30° angle to the corporeal axis. From this, Cinquemani theorized that the famous "figure 3" bloodstain on the forehead of the man on the Shroud was originally a bloodstained mark on the face resulting from a broken nose. At the moment of the Resurrection, Jesus' head position moved and the cloth stretched, thereby transferring the "figure 3" stain onto the forehead.

> It would have appeared on Christ's face when lowered by 10 cm on the vertical axis, it shows the central line of the figure 3 close to the left nasal pinna as blood from the left naris. A few minutes before the crucifixion a fall caused the wound to the right zigoma and the leftwards dislocation of the nasal cartilage. In the sepulchre the blood from the left naris had traced the "3" on the cloth and the drop that appears under the "3" on

> the left eyebrow. . . . The last drop had also soaked the corpse's left part of the moustache. . . . The arrow-head shaped clot visible on the hair to the top right, lowered on the vertical by 10 cm, appears with the tip corresponding to the zygomatic bone.[26]

The studies of Lavoie and Cinquemani support the "double image formation theory," namely, that the blood-stained image occurred prior to the body image.

## Pollen Tests

The results of tests for pollen on the Shroud are very interesting, yet still controversial.

Dr. Frei, who was present when the Shroud was examined in 1973 and 1978, took various sticky tape samples, enabling him to remove minute particles from the cloth. As a result of his study, he believed he was able to identify pollens from 58 different plants. Prior to his untimely death in 1983, Frei made seven trips to the Middle East in order to gather plant specimens to help him in his work of identifying pollens from the Shroud. Fr. Werner Bulst, S.J. commented:

> Pollens from 58 species of plants have been found on the Shroud. . . . [L]ess than one-third grow in France or Italy. . . . The small number of European species can be explained by the history of the Shroud in Europe, for, normally kept in a closed reliquary, the Shroud was protected from pollen contamination. Only on special occasions was it exposed in the open. . . . The spectrum of non-European species is highly astonishing. . . . There is only one place where all these plants—with the exception of three . . . grow in a very small radius: Jerusalem.[27]

# Table of Pollens from the Turin Shroud

## as Identified by Dr. Max Frei

Based on an original chart by Fr. Werner Bulst, S.J.

Origin of the plants whose pollens have been found on the Shroud: →

Alphabetical list of all the plants whose pollens have been found on the Shroud: ↓

| No. | Plant | France, Italy | Mediterranean Area | Istanbul Environs | Anatolian Steppe | Jerusalem & Environs | Iran-Turan | Arabia | Sahara | Regions of North Africa | Plant Description: |
|---|---|---|---|---|---|---|---|---|---|---|---|
| 1 | Acacia albida Del. | | | | | ● | | | | ● | Plant of deserts. Most frequent around the Dead Sea |
| 2 | Alnus glutinosa Vill. | ● | | | | | | | | | |
| 3 | Althaea officinalis L. | ● | ● | | | ● | | | | | Halophyte |
| 4 | Amaranthus lividius L. | ● | | | | | | | | | Love-lies-bleeding |
| 5 | Anabasis aphylla L. | | | | | ● | ● | ● | | ● | Plant of deserts, halophyte. Frequent in South Palestine |
| 6 | Anemone coronaria L. | | ● | | | ● | | | | | |
| 7 | Artemisia Herba-alba A. | | | | ● | ● | ● | ● | | ● | Plant of semideserts. Most frequent in east Jerusalem |
| 8 | Atraphaxis spinosa L. | | | | ● | | ● | | | | Plant of deserts, Iran, Turan, Anatolia |
| 9 | Bassia muricata Asch. | | | | | ● | | | | | |
| 10 | Capparis spec. | | ● | | ● | ● | ● | | | | Plant of semi-deserts. Frequent on rock debris & old walls (caper) |
| 11 | Carduus personata Jacq | ● | | | | | | | | | Thistle |
| 12 | Carpinus betulis L. | ● | | | | | | | | | |
| 13 | Cedrus libanotica Lk. | ● | ● | ● | | ● | | | | | Cedar of Lebanon |
| 14 | Cistus credicus L. | | ● | | | ● | | | | | Rock rose |
| 15 | Corylus avellana L. | ● | | ● | | | | | | | Hazel |
| 16 | Cupressus sempervirens L. | ● | ● | ● | | ● | | | | | Cypress |
| 17 | Echinops glaberrimus DC | | | | | ● | | | | ● | Plant of deserts. Frequent in rocky debris |
| 18 | Epimedium pubigerum DC | | | ● | | | | | | | Southeast Europe, Turkey |
| 19 | Fagonia mollis Del. | | | | | ● | | ● | ● | | Plant of deserts. Frequent in the valley of Jordan |
| 20 | Fagus silvatica L. | ● | | | | | | | | | Beech |
| 21 | Glaucium grandiflorum B&H | | | | ● | ● | ● | | | | Plant of steppes. Frequent in South Palestine |
| 22 | Gundelia Tournefortii L. | | | | ● | ● | ● | | | | Plant of salt steppes |
| 23 | Haloxylon persicum Bg. | | | | | ● | ● | | | | Plant of deserts, halophyte |
| 24 | Haplophyllum tuberculatum J. | | | | ● | ● | | ● | ● | | Plant of deserts |
| 25 | Helianthemum versicarium B. | | | | ● | ● | ● | | | ● | Plant of deserts & semideserts |
| 26 | Hyoscyamus aureus L. | | | | | ● | ● | | | | Plant frequent on rocks, old walls, ruins. Frequent on the old walls of Jerusalem |

| | Origin of the plants whose pollens have been found on the Shroud: → Alphabetical list of all the plants whose pollens have been found on the Shroud: ↓ | France, Italy | Mediterranean Area | Istanbul Environs | Anatolian Steppe | Jerusalem & Environs | Iran-Turan | Arabia | Sahara | Regions of North Africa | Plant Description: ↓ |
|---|---|---|---|---|---|---|---|---|---|---|---|
| 27 | Hyoscyamus reticulatus L. | | | | ● | ● | ● | | | | Plant of steppes. Frequent on ruins. |
| 28 | Ixiolirion montanum Herb | | | | ● | ● | | | | | Plant of steppes. |
| 29 | Juniperus oxycedrus L. | | ● | ● | | ● | ● | | | | Coniferous evergreen shrub (Juniper) |
| 30 | Laurus nobilis L. | ● | ● | ● | | ● | | | | | Laurel |
| 31 | Linum mucronatum Bert. | | | | ● | ● | ● | | | | Plant of limy steppes. |
| 32 | Lythrum salicaria L. | ● | | | | | | | | | |
| 33 | Oligomejus subulata Boiss. | | | ● | | ● | ● | | | ● | Plant of sandy and limy deserts |
| 34 | Onosma syriacum Labill. | | | | | ● | ● | | | | Plant of steppes and deserts. Frequently on the walls of old Jerusalem |
| 35 | Oryza sativa L. | ● | | | | | | | | | Rice |
| 36 | Paliurus Spina-Christi Mill. | | ● | | | ● | ● | | | | |
| 37 | Peganum Harmala L. | | | | ● | ● | ● | | | ● | Plant of deserts. |
| 38 | Phyllirea angustifolia L. | | ● | | | ● | | | | | |
| 39 | Pinus halepensis L. | | ● | | | ● | | | | | Pine |
| 40 | Pistacia lentiscus L. | | ● | | | ● | | | | | Pistacia |
| 41 | Pistacia vera L. | | ● | | | ● | | | | | Pistacia |
| 42 | Plantanus orientalis L. | ● | ● | ● | ● | ● | ● | | | | Oriental plane tree |
| 43 | Poterium spinosum L. | | ● | ● | | ● | | | | | Plant of arid soils |
| 44 | Prosopis farcta Macbr. | | | | ● | ● | ● | | | | Most frequent around the Dead Sea |
| 45 | Prunus spartioides Spach. | | | | ● | | | | | | |
| 46 | Pteranthus dichotomus Forsk | | | | ● | ● | ● | | | ● | Plant of sand and limy deserts |
| 47 | Reaumuria hirtella J&Sp | | | | | ● | ● | ● | ● | | Plant of salt steppes |
| 48 | Rieinus communis L. | ● | ● | ● | ● | ● | | | | | Plant of steppes (castor-oil plants) |
| 49 | Ridolfia segetum moris | | ● | | | ● | | | | | |
| 50 | Roemeria hybrida (L)DC | | | ● | ● | ● | ● | | | | Plant of steppes |
| 51 | Scabiosa prolifera L. | | | | ● | ● | | | | ● | Plant of arid soils |
| 52 | Scirpus triquertrus L. | ● | | ● | | ● | | | | | Rush |
| 53 | Secale spec. | ● | | | | | | | | | Rye |
| 54 | Silene conoida L. | | ● | | ● | ● | ● | | | | Plant of steppes |
| 55 | Suaeda aegyptiaca Zoh. | | | | | ● | | ● | ● | | Plant of salt steppes |
| 56 | Tamarix nilotica Bunge | | | | | ● | | ● | ● | | Plant of salt steppes |
| 57 | Taxus baccata L. | ● | | ● | | | | | | | Yew |
| 58 | Zygophyllum dumosum B. | | | | | ● | | | ● | | Plant of deserts. Most frequent around the Dead Sea |
| | **Total Numbers** | **17** | **18** | **13** | **18** | **45** | **22** | **7** | **6** | **9** | |

Some critics denigrated Frei's work and accused him of being an amateur scientist because he used an inexpensive department-store tape dispenser to take his samples rather than the scientific torque applicator. Of the thirty-four sample tapes taken by Rogers, STURP was only able to identify one pollen from a ragweed that grows prodigiously in Turin.[28] Perhaps the reason Frei was able to pick up more pollens than STURP was that he applied great pressure when he placed his sticky tape to the cloth.

In a letter dated April 20, 1984, Dr. Heller remarked: "Frei's data are null and useless."[29] He continued:

> Pollen is transported by the air very far, over very great distances, thousands of kilometers. If you consult a map of the east coast of the United States, you will see that the north of New York State is about 2000 kilometers [1240 miles] from the north of the Florida headland. Now there grows in the north of the Florida headland, and there only, a kind of cypress which gives pollens at a certain precise time of the year. Well, at the same moment, a deposit of these pollens in great quantity is to be observed as far as the north of New York State. . . .
>
> Pollens coming from the mainland have been detected in the middle of the Atlantic Ocean. Pollen particles from the Sahara and its borderland can be found in Florida counter to the prevailing winds, which do not blow in this direction. In the Mediterranean, air currents and also storms transport pollens from the Near East to the south of Europe.[30]

Frei rebutted his critics by saying:

> Plants on the Shroud from Palestine and Anatolia are so numerous, compared to the species

> from Europe, that a casual contamination or a pollen-transport from the Near East by storms in different seasons cannot be responsible for their presence. . . . The predominance of these pollens must be the result of the Shroud's stay in such countries. . . .[31]

Dr. Whanger and his wife Mary have supported Frei. They responded to comments regarding pollens being carried by the wind, saying: "That is hardly likely, as many of these pollens are heavy pollens with prickly surfaces designed to be carried by insects, not by wind."[32] Even if one were to admit that the pollens were airborne, it would be highly coincidental that they were from areas where the Shroud has been alleged to have traveled.

Giovanni Riggi, the microanalyst who participated in the 1978 examination of the Shroud, doubts the reliability of Frei's research. He writes:

> In fact, nearly all the pollens found on the adhesive tapes in America and those found in a great number by myself in among the dust, defied any kind of recognition, because they were covered in incrustation causing their characteristic forms and aspects to deteriorate. In order to discover the hidden surface of each of them, inserted in amongst a host of other mineral and biological particles, it was and remains necessary to open the crust of the covering chemically. But on coming into contact with acid, it would be eroded together with all the other surrounding elements.[33]

According to Wilson, one reason why the pollen samples taken by Riggi were unidentifiable was that he took his samples from the underside of the Shroud, which would have been in direct contact with the stone in the tomb. If this were so, the calcium-coated surface of the rock would have affected the distinctive features of the pollens.[34]

Perhaps the most important discovery made by Frei concerns spores from halophyte, plants which thrive in salty soil and are unique to desert regions near the Dead Sea. Frei states:

> These plants are of great diagnostic value for our geographical studies as identical desert plants are missing in all the other countries where the Shroud is believed to have been exposed to the open air. Consequently, a forgery, produced somewhere in France during the Middle Ages, in a country lacking these typical halophytes, could not contain such characteristic pollen grains from the desert regions of Palestine.[35]

In 1988, twenty-seven samples from Frei's pollen collection were acquired by the Association of Scientists and Scholars International for the Shroud of Turin (ASSIST) founded by Paul Maloney. At a workshop on the study of pollen at the Philadelphia Academy of Natural Sciences, Dr. McCrone affirmed that the pollens collected by Frei were indeed from the Shroud.[36]

## Pontius Pilate Coins

Shortly after obtaining three-dimensional photos of the Shroud in 1977, Dr. Jackson and Dr. Jumper detected small objects like buttons in the eye sockets of the face on the Shroud. Similar findings were later made in 1978 by Professor Tamburelli. In 1979, Fr. Francis Filas, S.J., a theologian, mathematician and physicist at Loyola University in Chicago, studied enlarged photographs of the eyes of the man on the Shroud and discovered what appeared to be a coin on the right eye (coins were often placed on the eyelids of a corpse to keep them closed). The diameter of the coin was 15 mm, which was the same size as those struck under the reign of Pontius Pilate. Fr. Filas noticed four letters, YCAI, around a curved staff. It is known that the astrologer's staff was the emblem of Pilate. The four letters formed part of the Greek inscription: TIBEPIO(Y) KAICAPOC, i.e., "Of Tiberius Caesar." Sometimes in transliteration the letter "C" would be substituted for "K" and the letter "Y" for "U" which is actually the Greek letter *upsilon* with a tail. (Mistakes in spelling were also common as coins were die cast by hand.) According to Fr. Filas: "If true, it could date the shroud to between 29 and 36 A.D. in a way no other scientific method could."[37]

What concerned Fr. Filas, however, was the substitution of the Latin "C" for the Greek "K." This led him to search out ancient coins of the period, and he actually found one with a similar misspelling. Another explanation for the "misspelling" is that the vertical bar of the Greek letter *kappa* (K) was detached when the image was transferred to the cloth. In 1983, Fr. Filas sent his coin and photos to be reviewed by Dr. Robert Haralick, Director of the Spatial Data Analysis Laboratory of Virginia Polytechnic Institute. Cautiously optimistic, he stated, "The evidence is definitely supporting evidence, because there is some degree of match between what one would expect to find if the Shroud did indeed contain a faint image of the Pilate coin and what we can in fact observe in the original and in the digitally processed images."[38]

When Fr. Filas died on February 15, 1985, his pioneer research regarding the coins on the Shroud was later confirmed by others. Mario Moroni, an Italian numismatist, asserts that what Fr. Filas interpreted as the letter "C" on the coin was actually part of the astrologer's staff.[39]

Later, the Whangers obtained photos of Fr. Filas' coin and compared them with the enlarged photos of the eyes on the Shroud using their polarized image overlay technique. They commented that

> comparing the same area on the 1931 and 1978 photographs, this technique shows that the cloth is not in exactly the same position and drape for the two photographs and that threads over the eye area might have been stretched or rotated. This accounts for some apparent distortion of the letters and images in the 1978 photographs indeed making it more difficult to see them on these photographs.[40]

Using photos from numismatic books, the Whangers were able to identify the Filas coin as being one struck during the reign of Tiberius in A.D. 29:

> We identified three tiny letters: L (signifies that the letters following have numerical value), I (number value of ten), and a letter called Stigma that looks something like a rounded number five that was at that time becoming obsolete (number value of six). Thus the coin was dated to the sixteenth year of the reign of Tiberius Caesar, which is A.D. 29.[41]

The dating of coins in ancient times was based upon the regnal year of the emperor, not the calendar year. In addition, Greek letters were used for numbers. The Whangers also found that this coin had 211 points of congruence with the object over the right eye of the Shroud and 86 points of discordance.[42] Although the features of the coin over the left eye are not as clear as those of the right, the researchers were nonetheless able to identify that coin as the Julia lepton. A lepton is a small copper coin equivalent to a "widow's mite." This coin was struck in 29 A.D. in honor of Tiberius' mother, Julia. Again, using the polarized image overlay technique, the Whangers were able to count 73 points of congruence between the object on the left eye of the Shroud and the Julia lepton.[43]

In 1996, Professor Bollone and Professor Nello Balossino, a computer expert, both from the University of Turin, confirmed the presence of coins on the eyes. They reported that the coin on the left eye was higher, probably due to facial swelling. Perhaps this is the reason the Whangers were initially unable to ascertain its features. Traces of the coin on the left eye are identical with those of one kept at the British Museum which was minted during the reign of Tiberius. Professor Bollone emphatically states: "No more must we rely on tests or calculations; we now have an 'intrinsic' proof, clearly stamped, as it were, upon the Shroud itself. No medieval forger could have accomplished this. . . . In my opinion, this latest research is just about 100% proof that the Shroud of Turin truly held the body of the crucified and buried Christ."[44]

If the images on the eyes are in fact coins, the question raised is, how were they superimposed on the cloth? In the fall of 1982, after viewing coin overlay photos by Dr. Whanger, Dr. Adler observed that the image had emerged from the raised points of the coin, not the smooth surface. This high energy phenomenon is associated with corona discharge. As the Whangers point out, "In a corona discharge, ionizing electrical energy first spreads over the surface of any object in the electrical field, whatever it may be—flesh, hair, cloth, leather, metal, etc. The sparks or ions then tend to be discharged as streamers which may be two inches or more in length."[45]

There is no consensus among Shroud experts that coins are present over the eyes. The 1931 and 1978 photos of the same area of the eye indicate that the cloth may have stretched or been rotated, thus altering the image. It has been suggested that the supposed "coins" are a result of the weave patterns in the cloth, giving the effect of letters on a lepton. Rebecca Jackson, wife of Dr. Jackson and a Jewish ethnologist who converted to Christianity in 1987 and to Catholicism in 1991, maintains that Jews would not put coins of pagans on the eyes of a corpse because images are forbidden by the Talmud. But the Whangers state that the lepton of Pontius Pilate was actually a Jewish coin struck in a Roman province.[46] According to Dr. Kindler, former director of the museum Haaretz in Tel Aviv, only Roman coins were struck in Judea between 6 and 66 A.D.[47] Jackson says that if there is anything on the eyes it would most likely be potsherds.

## Early Portraits of the Holy Face

Sacred Scripture does not provide us with any physical description of Jesus. People of the first century were more concerned with His message than with what He looked like. Representations of Christ prior to the sixth century varied. Most often He was portrayed as a young beardless man with short hair. Around the sixth century, a common representation of the face of Christ with long hair, mustache and beard began to emerge and has been a standard depiction ever since.

Perhaps the first person to notice this gradual change was Paul Vignon in the 1930s. He was later followed by Fr. Wuenschel. These researchers noticed a number of similarities between the face on the Shroud and early paintings and icons of Christ, particularly in the Byzantine tradition. They identified about twenty unusual details. Some of the most notable are the two strands of hair at the top of the forehead. Particularly noteworthy is the directionality of the wisps of hair, which is to the right, just like the bloodstain on the Shroud in the form of the Greek letter *epsilon* when viewed with the naked eye. The bloodstain only appears as the number "3" on a negative photo of the Shroud. Other parallels include a three-sided "square" between the brows (believed by some to be caused by a phylactery, a small leather box containing Scripture parchments worn around the forehead by Jewish men—cf. *Deut.* 6:8); an enlarged left nostril; a "V" shape at the bridge of the nose; one eyebrow higher than the other; a transverse line across the throat (perhaps a crease from the way the Shroud was folded); and a forked beard.[48] These facial characteristics found on the Shroud appear in most images of the face of Christ as early as the sixth century. Another interesting point is that artists who painted copies of the image usually depicted the face in a frame surrounded by an ornamental trellis. This may very well have been the way in which the face on the Shroud was displayed for veneration. Ian Wilson surmises that there must have been an official "portrait" which was used by artists as a model for their paintings.

Dr. Whanger and his wife used their polarized image overlay technique to compare the face on the Shroud with that on two Byzantine gold solidi coins minted between 692 and 695 A.D. under the reign of Justinian II. This was the first coin which bore the portrait of Jesus. The Shroud face and the coins were photographed with the same proportions on transparencies and then projected upon one another. The face on the coins measured between eight and nine millimeters in height from the crown of the head to the tip of the beard. On the first coin, the Whangers found approximately 145 points of congruence, including minute details such as bloodstains, small markings and even wrinkles on the Shroud that were replicated on the coin. The second coin had 105 points of congruence.[49] This is a significant discovery given that in a court of law, only 14 points of congruence are needed to establish the same fingerprints, and between 45 and 60 points of congruence are sufficient to determine the same face.[50]

In 1979, a colleague of Dr. Whanger who was doing research at the Monastery of St. Catherine at Mt. Sinai brought back photos of icons in the monastery. One of them was of Christ the Pantocrator (Almighty), dating back to the sixth century. When Whanger's friend asked a monk about the origin of the image, the monk replied that it had been copied from the Shroud of Turin.[51] Whanger's interest in this icon was piqued, and he decided to use his polarized image overlay technique to compare the face of the icon with that of the Shroud. He found over 200 points of congruence between the two, "including such features as a tear running down from the left eye, small irregular areas on the lips, and configurations of lines in the halo or nimbus. . . . This astonishing fidelity between the Pantocrator icon and the Shroud would indicate that the artist had direct access to the Shroud image when the icon was produced."[52]

Given that early portraits of Christ depicted the face only, and the cloth known as the Mandylion was in all probability the Shroud framed in such a manner as to expose the face alone, artists may have been actually inspired by the Shroud for their paintings. It is only around the eleventh century that a full-length frontal and dorsal representation of Christ began to appear.

## Pilgrim's Medallion

A fortuitous discovery which adds another piece to the case for the Shroud's historicity concerns a pilgrim's medallion dating from about 1357 which was found in the Seine River in Paris in 1855 by Arthur Forgeais. This small lead object, most likely a souvenir of a pilgrim's visit, is now kept in the Museum of Cluny. It depicts the frontal and dorsal image of a body on a long sheet being held out for veneration by two clerics vested in copes. It is obvious that the heads are broken. The image is an uncanny replica of what is now known as the Shroud of Turin. The double body image depicts a naked figure with crossed hands and trickles of blood on the back and feet. As an added touch of realism one can also detect the herringbone weave pattern that appears on the Shroud.

Of striking note are the two coats of arms represented on the reliquary beneath the Shroud on the medallion. The one on the left (as viewed by reader) is that of Geoffrey I de Charny, represented with three small inner shields. The original would have been silver on a red background. The one on the right is that of Jeanne de Vergy, represented with three flowers which would have been gold. Flanked between the coats of arms are the instruments of the Passion. Clearly visible are the flagrum, the scourging column, the lance, nails, and, in the middle of the two shields, a roundel symbolizing the empty tomb surmounted by a cross upon which is hung a crown of thorns.

Although the exact date or origin of the medal is not certain, the coats of arms give us a clue. Since Geoffrey I de Charny was Lord of Lirey, the medallion probably came from that region. Humbert de Villersexel, the second husband of Marguerite de Charny, to whom various relics were entrusted for safekeeping in 1418, acknowledged receiving "a cloth, on which is the figure or representation of the Shroud of our Lord Jesus Christ, which is in a casket emblazoned with the de Charny crest." Geoffrey I de Charny died on September 19, 1356; therefore, it is highly unlikely that his crest would have been engraved on a medallion produced after that year.

## The Pray Manuscript

In his book on the history of the Shroud of Turin, a Dominican priest, Fr. Andre M. Dubarle, O.P. remarked that an image of the Shroud appears in the first extant book in the Hungarian language. This manuscript is known as the Pray Manuscript or Codex, named after Georgius Pray, who discovered it in the eighteenth century.[53] This codex, kept at the Budapest National Library, is believed to have been written between 1192 and 1195 because of the historical details it relates. The manuscript contains four pen and ink drawings pertaining to the death of Jesus. The first panel depicts the Crucifixion; the second shows the descent from the Cross with Joseph of Arimathea and Nicodemus holding the body of Jesus while the Virgin Mary holds His head; the third panel is divided into two, the top section showing the body of Jesus laid out on a cloth for burial, and the lower section depicting the arrival of the holy women on Easter morn who find an angel at the empty tomb; and the fourth panel is that of the glorified Christ.

The French geneticist Dr. Jerome Lejeune delivered a paper at a conference in 1993 in which he discussed the Pray Manuscript. (Shortly before his death on Easter 1994, Dr. Lejeune had been appointed by Pope John Paul II as the founding chairman of the Pontifical Academy for Life.) He remarked that the artist's attention to details suggested he was familiar with the image on the Shroud. Lejeune noted the following common characteristics between the Pray Manuscript and the Shroud.[54]

- The Shroud was twice the length of a man.
- The Shroud has a herringbone weave.
- The cloth had L-shaped hole marks on the front and back.
- Jesus wore a beard and long hair.
- There is a scar above the right eye corresponding to the "3"-shaped bloodstain on the Shroud.
- The body was completely naked.
- The right hand was laid over the left.
- The fingers were unnaturally elongated, and the thumbs invisible.
- The wound on the left hand is in the palm, but on the right hand the wound is on the wrist.
- One panel shows only three nails used for crucifixion.

One of the most minute yet most revealing similarities between the Pray Manuscript and the Shroud of Turin is what Wilson refers to as the "poker holes" on the Shroud. These two parallel groups of small puncture-like burn marks are located near the hands of the man on the Shroud and on the dorsal image on each side of the man's thighs. On the panel of the codex depicting the arrival of the three holy women, similar "poker holes" formed like an inverted, upside down "L" can be seen on the top sheet which represents the Shroud partly folded over. Other small holes can be seen on the bottom part of the cloth between little red Greek crosses representing bloodstains.

According to Fr. Dubarle, these puncture-like burn marks were probably caused by sparks from a censer. Wilson suggests that they were caused by some sort of test for authenticity using a red hot poker, perhaps when the Shroud was supposedly subjected to a "trial by fire" in 1503. In all likelihood these burn marks were caused by pitch, which can be detected near the holes. Evidence of these "poker holes" pre-dating the 1532 fire can be seen on a copy of the Shroud reportedly made by Albrecht Dürer in 1516 and kept at the Church of St. Gommaire in Lier, Belgium. Tests conducted on the Shroud of Turin by Vern Miller in 1978 showed that the burn marks of the 1532 fire fluoresce due to the fact that the fire occurred in a closed box. The burn marks of an earlier fire did not fluoresce, possibly because the fire took place in open air with ample supply of oxygen.

In the words of Dr. Lejeune: "The artist who produced the Codex of Pray had before his eyes . . . a model that possessed all of the unique characteristics of the Shroud of Turin."[55]

## Inscriptions on the Shroud?

In 1978, Piero Ugolotti, a pharmacist and amateur student of the Shroud, was examining photos of the image taken by Cordiglia and noticed writings around the face of the man.[56] He then contacted Monsignor Aldo Marastoni, a renowned paleologist, papyrologist and philologist at the Catholic University in Milan, who examined the photographs, as well as reproductions of Enrie's, and discovered inscriptions written in Hebrew, Greek and Latin. At least three Hebrew letters can be discerned above the right eyebrow (the left on a photographic negative). These letters are: Tau, Vau (which can also be construed as a Jod because of the uncertain downstroke), and Sade. The meaning of these letters is unclear but they probably constitute the final ending of a Hebrew or Aramaic phrase, because the word is followed by a punctuation mark which some interpret as being a possible fourth letter, Lamed.

In the center of the forehead can be seen traces of two fragments of a word in lapidary Latin. They appear to be a double impression of the same signs. One part consists of the letters "IB" and is lower and slightly to the right, and the other part with the letters "IBER" is higher and slightly towards the center. The final "R" is uncertain, out of line and slanted to the right. It is very tempting to read "IB-IBER" as the residue of the name Tiberius Caesar.

On the left side of the face (i.e., the right on a photographic negative), progressing from the bottom upwards, one can read in uncial italics characteristic of the first century A.D. the words "INN ECE," with the double "N" attached. Actually, it is "IN NECEM" ("to death"), but the final "M" was often omitted in the vernacular. This same phrase is repeated in reverse on a horizontal line under the chin and also to the left of the face (right on a photographic negative) from the top down. The triple repetition of this death sentence of the condemned calls to mind the *titulus* placed above the head of Christ on the Cross written in Hebrew, Latin and Greek (cf. *John* 15:20).

Looking at a three-dimensional photograph of the face one can see on the right side of the photographic negative descending from top to bottom and juxtaposed to "INNECE" the following capital letters:

"S N AZARE." The "S" appears to be the ending part of a word, then there is a space followed by an "N", and another space in which can be seen traces of an "E", followed by the remaining letters. It is clear that these fragment letters form the word "Nazarenus."

How and why were these inscriptions formed and placed

on the Shroud? Marastoni says that one has to exclude the possibility that these graphic signs are a random convergence of various letters. He proposes the theory of a "mitre" or some sort of hood (such as an executioner's hood) being placed on the head of the condemned man.[57] This hood would have been made of a permeable material with the death sentence inscribed on it. The writing would have transferred onto the man's skin as a result of his sweat. This hypothesis is not very convincing because there is no mention of such a hood in the Gospels. Jesus' head was crowned with thorns, thereby making a direct contact of a hood to His forehead improbable. Furthermore, the Gospels relate that Jesus spoke from the Cross and looked at those around Him; therefore, His head was uncovered. With regard to the inscriptions around the face, Marastoni suggests that a type of "fork" in the shape of a "U" was placed under the man's chin and attached to the *patibulum* of the cross.[58] At first glance this theory seems more probable than the other; however, in the Gospel of John we are told that when Jesus died He bowed His head and gave up His spirit (*John* 19:30). This would not have been possible if His head were held in position by a "fork" attached to the Cross.

Subsequent studies by other researchers have found additional inscriptions on the Shroud. Roberto Messina, a medical-legal professional and an expert in Hebrew, along with Carlo Orecchia, a professor of biblical Hebrew in Milan, concur with Ugolotti and Marastoni that there are signs written on the cloth. However, they propose a different interpretation of the characters above the right eyebrow (left on a photographic negative). They also notice traces of a second and a third word above the left eyebrow which are in a symetrical position to the first. They suggest two possible readings: *milk hw'hyhwdym* or *mich dy hyhwddyn*, both of which signify "(this is) the king of the Jews."[59]

In 1995, Gregoire Kaplan, Marcel Alonso and Andre Marion, working in collaboration with the *Institut d' Optique d'Orsay* of Paris, confirmed the presence of writings around the face of the man on the Shroud. In a presentation of their study in 1997, Andre Marion and Anne-Laure Courage candidly admitted that the graphics on the Shroud are very obscure and that the photographs can report diverse information depending upon the condition and procedures in which they were carried out and developed.[60]

Some of the writings they found include: PEZω, which in ancient Greek has the connotation of "to complete" as in a sacrificial sense; there is also ψΣKIA, which could have been part of the word ΩψΣKIA, meaning "shadow of a face" or "a face barely visible," and under the chin there are the letters HΣOγ that could be part of IHΣOγ or "Jesus."[61]

The researchers maintain that in general the classical form of the characters indicate an eastern origin of an era prior to the fifth century, while the two attached Ns suggest a western origin of an era between the eighth and twelfth centuries. The form of the Σ used is found in epigraphs of the second century and was rarely used in the Middle Ages. According to Marion and Courage, "The difficulty of the readings, the extreme simplicity of the signs and the manner in which the characters were 'affixed,' render all conclusions uncertain as to the epoch in which the inscriptions were marked."[62]

The presence of inscriptions on the Shroud first discovered by Ugolotti and Marastoni is indeed intriguing and merits further research into this area. If it can be proved with certainty that the writings antedate the Middle Ages, we have further evidence of the authenticity of the cloth as the Shroud of Christ.

## The Devil and the Shroud

The Russians have a saying: "Wherever Christians build a church the devil pitches his tent across the street." This is particularly true with regard to the city of Turin, where the Shroud, believed by many to have enveloped the body of the crucified Christ, is housed.

During the second half of the nineteenth century, Turin became a refuge for a number of magicians and those involved with the occult. These were turbulent times of great opposition between Church and state. In order to undermine the Catholic Church, governors of Piedmont allowed greater freedom to satanists and occultists. Satanic sects gradually began to disappear in Turin after adherents of such sects were first put to trial in 1890. According to Massimo Introvigne, a sociologist from Turin, the phenomenon all but disappeared in the 1960s.[63] But did it?

In a general audience on November 15, 1972, Pope Paul VI spoke of "that evil which is called the Devil," and said "evil is not merely a lack of something, but an effective agent, a living, spiritual being, perverted and perverting." Many wished he had not spoken on the subject. Progressives and liberals thought it was a return to the so-called "Dark Ages" characterized by plagues and witchcraft. While the mention of the devil and evil is mocked by those who consider themselves the enlightened of our day, there is an umbra casting its darkness on our age which goes unnoticed. We have plagues of which we know the cause but not the cure, there are self-professed witches teaching in colleges, and there are psychics advertising on television.

Although the practice of occultism has risen throughout the world, there seems to be a disproportionate number of satanists centered in Turin—the figures reported are as high as 40,000. In the mid-1980s, Cardinal Anastasio Ballestrero, the Archbishop of Turin, tripled the number of exorcists in his diocese due to the increase in the number of exorcisms being performed.[64] Is this merely due to the history of satanists gravitating to this region, or could it be due to the presence of the Holy Shroud, which is a constant reminder of Jesus' triumph over Satan's chains of sin and death?

In September 1988, Pope John Paul II visited Turin on the occasion of the centennial anniversary of the death of St. John Bosco. During a luncheon with bishops of Piedmont, the Pope remarked, "Where there are saints, there enters also another who does not present himself by his own name but under other names. He is called the Prince of this world, the devil."[65]

## –9–

# 1988 Carbon-14 Controversy

ON October 13, 1988, Cardinal Ballestrero, the Pontifical Custodian of the Shroud, issued the following press release regarding the Carbon-14 test performed on the cloth:

> In a dispatch received by the Pontifical Custodian of the Holy Shroud on 28 September 1988, the laboratories of the University of Arizona, of the University of Oxford, and of the Polytechnic of Zurich which had conducted the tests for the radiocarbon dating of the cloth of the Holy Shroud, have finally communicated the result of their tests through Dr. Tite of the British Museum, the Coordinator of the project.
>
> This document states that the cloth of the Shroud can be assigned with a confidence of ninety-five percent accuracy to a date between A.D. 1260 and 1390. More precise and detailed information concerning the result will be published by the laboratories and Dr. Tite in a scientific review in an article which is in course of preparation.
>
> For his part, Prof. Bray of the "G. Colonnetti" Institute of Metrology of Turin, who was charged with the review of the summary report presented by Dr. Tite, has confirmed the compatibility of the results obtained by the three laboratories, whose certainty falls within the limits envisaged by the methods used.

After having informed the Holy See, the owner of the Holy Shroud, I make known what has been communicated to me. In submitting to science the evaluation of these results, the Church confirms her respect and veneration for this venerable icon of Christ, which remains an object of devotion for the faithful in keeping with the attitude always expressed in regard to the Holy Shroud, namely, that the value of the image is more important than the date of the Shroud itself. This attitude disposes of the gratuitous deductions of a theological character advanced in the sphere of a research which had been presented as solely and rigorously scientific.

At the same time the problems about the origin of the image and its preservation still remain to a large extent unresolved and will require further research and study. In regard to this the Church will show the same openness, inspired by the love of truth which she showed by permitting the radiocarbon dating as soon as she was presented with a reasonable and effective programme in regard to that matter.

I personally regret the deplorable fact that many reports concerning this scientific research were anticipated in the press, especially of the English language, because it also favoured the by no means objective insinuation that the Church was afraid of science by trying to conceal its results, an accusation in open contradiction to the Church's attitude on this occasion also when she has gone ahead resolutely.

Turin, 13 October 1988
Cardinal Anastasio Ballestrero[1]

The general public assumed from the Cardinal's statement that the Church was acknowledging that the Shroud is a fake. In fact, after the communique, it was common to read headlines with words such as "hoax," "forgery" and "medieval fake." For many, the Carbon-14 test was an infallible scientific pronouncement that should be accepted without question. For others, the results of the test were an anomaly, for studies up to 1988 seemed to indicate that the Shroud was authentic. Unfortunately, a great segment of the populace readily discounted data from various other disciplines in favor of the Carbon-14 dating.

## What Is Carbon-14 Dating?

Carbon-14 testing was developed by the chemist Willard F. Libby from the University of Chicago between 1946 and 1955. It is a method of determining when a living creature or plant died. Most carbon, 98.89% of that in natural living beings, is Carbon-12, and 1.11% is comprised of Carbon-13. Both of these isotopes are stable, meaning they retain their electrons. Carbon-14, on the other hand, is unstable and radioactive, originating in the high atmosphere from the bombardment of nitrogen atoms by neutrons. There is about one C-14 atom for every trillion C-12 atoms. While an organism is alive, there is a constant ratio between C-12 and C-14. However, when an organism dies, C-14 begins to decay at a fixed rate. Libby originally calculated that it takes 5,568 years for Carbon-14 to be reduced by half. This time period was later extended to 5,730 years. Carbon-14 continues to be reduced by half with each succeeding 5,730 years. Therefore, by measuring the amount of C-14 remaining in an object, one can determine its age. Apropos of the Shroud, by calculating the date in which the flax used to make the linen died, one can ascertain the age of the cloth. To do this, part of the material needs to be destroyed.

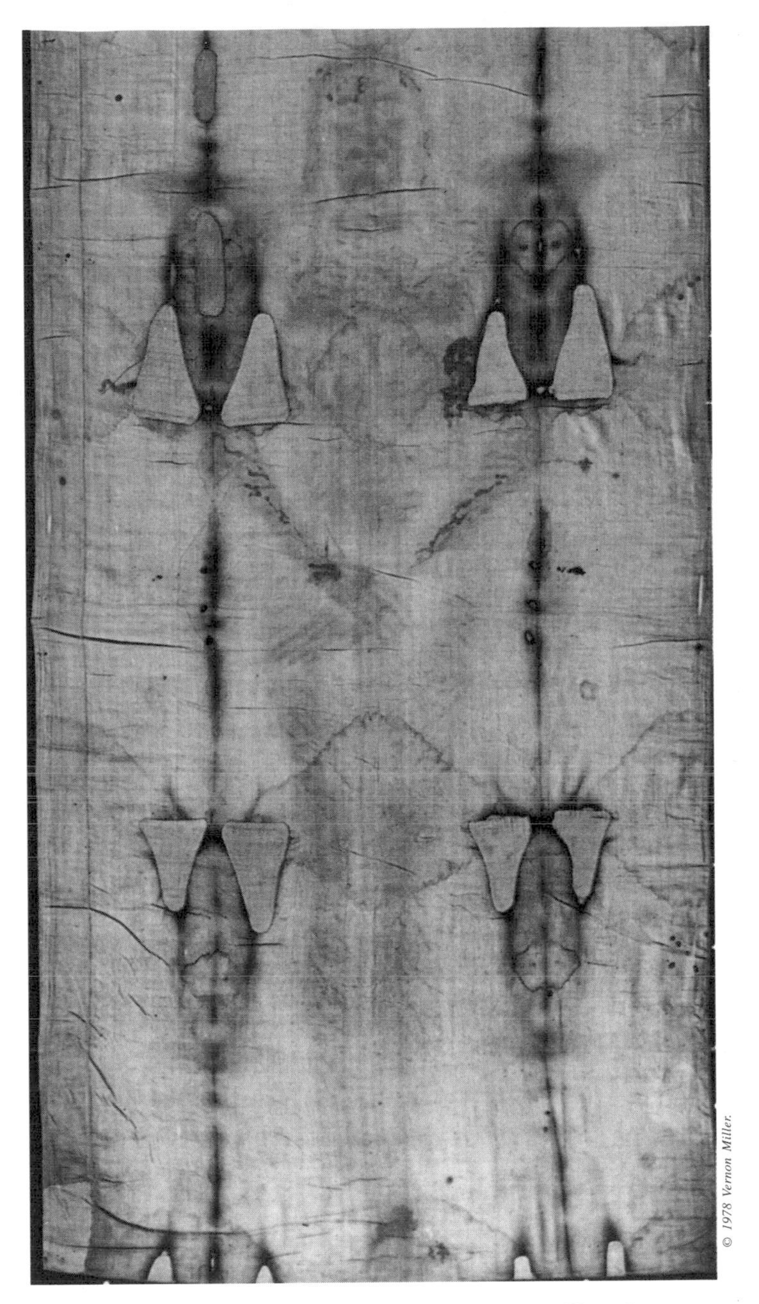


Complete frontal image of the man on the Shroud.

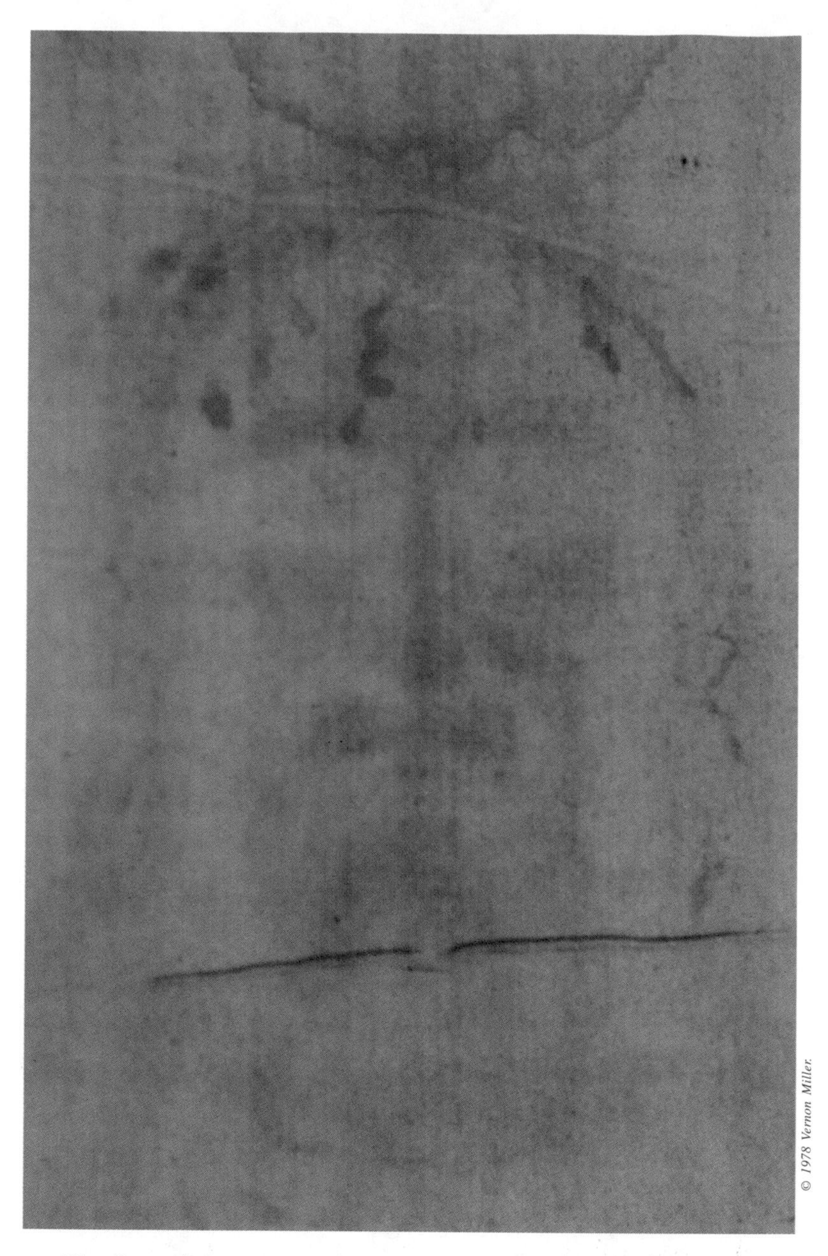


The face of the man on the Shroud as viewed with unaided eye.

Photographic negative of the face of the man on the Shroud. Note that the negative yields a "positive" image. This was the great discovery made in 1898 when the Shroud was first photographed.

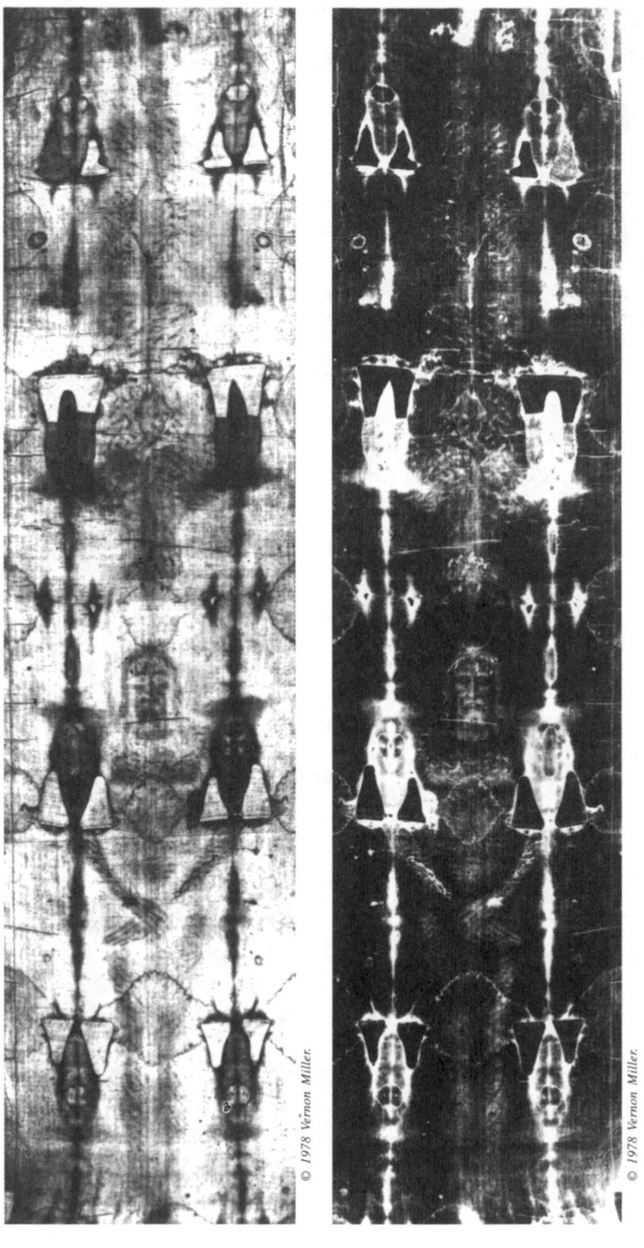


Photographic positive. Photographic negative.

Two full-length views of the Shroud.

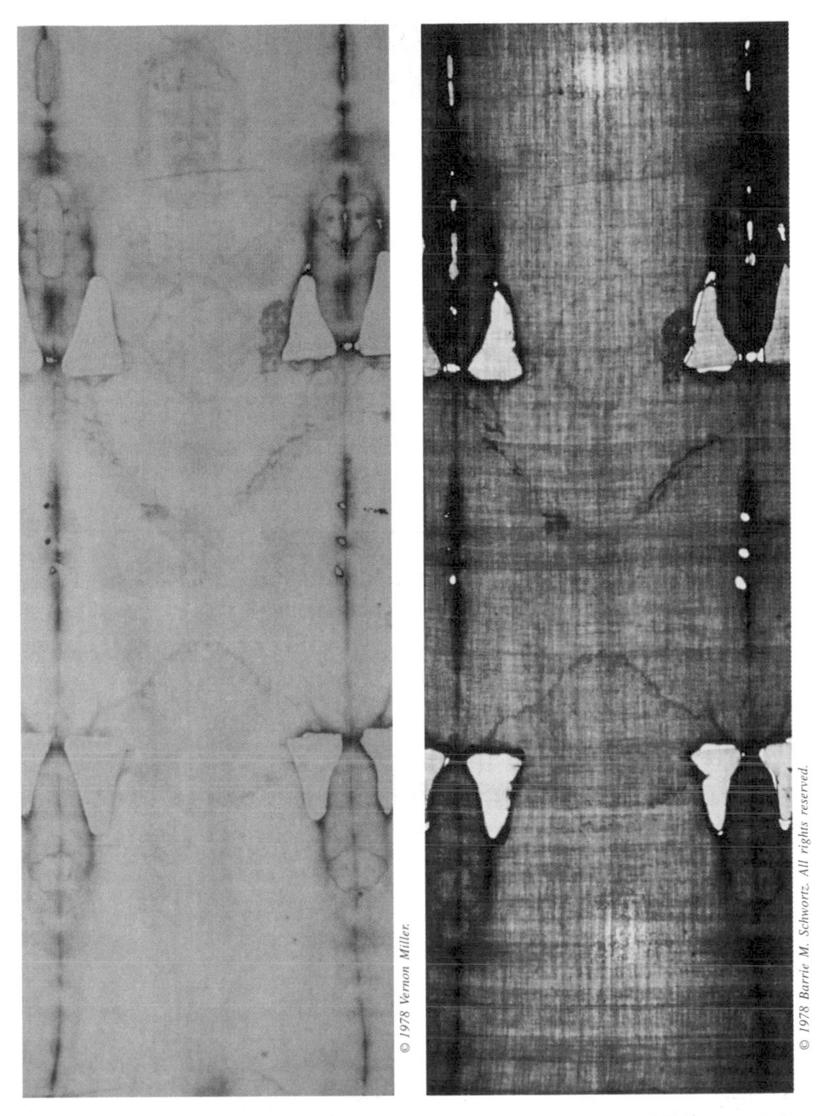


*Left*: Frontal portion of the Shroud as viewed with the unaided eye. *Right*: Frontal portion of the Shroud as viewed in transmitted light (that is, lighted from behind). Notice how the body image seems to disappear. This indicates that the image appears only on the linen's surface fibers.

Courtesy, Centro Español de Sindonologia.

The Sudarium, believed to be the face cloth which was used to cover the face of Jesus when He was taken down from the cross (*John* 20:6-7). The cloth has been kept in the Cathedral of Oviedo, Spain, since the eleventh century.

Courtesy, Centro Español de Sindonologia.

The Arca Santa, which houses the Sudarium.

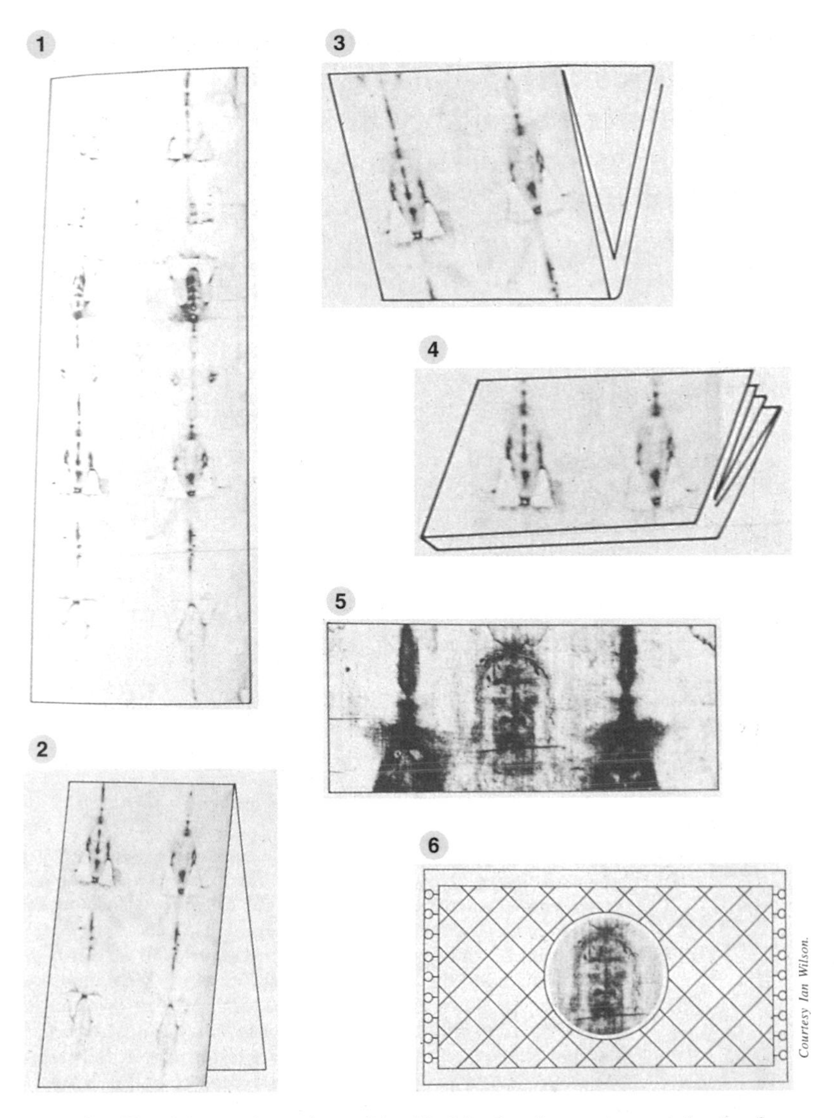


How the Shroud may have been "doubled in four" to expose only the face as the Mandylion:

1) The full length Shroud. 2) The Shroud doubled. 3) The Shroud folded again into four sections, approximately 43 inches. 4) The Shroud folded another time into eight sections, approximately 21½ inches. 5) How the Shroud face appears "doubled in four." 6) How the Shroud face would have been displayed in a case with a trellis-like cover as the Image of Edessa.

*Photo, Maurizio Paolicchi.*

Hungarian Pray Manuscript (c. 1192–1195). The illustration shows the entombment of Jesus. Notice the crossed hands and missing thumbs as on the Shroud. Also, there are tiny "poker holes" representing burn marks on the Shroud which pre-date the 1532 fire.

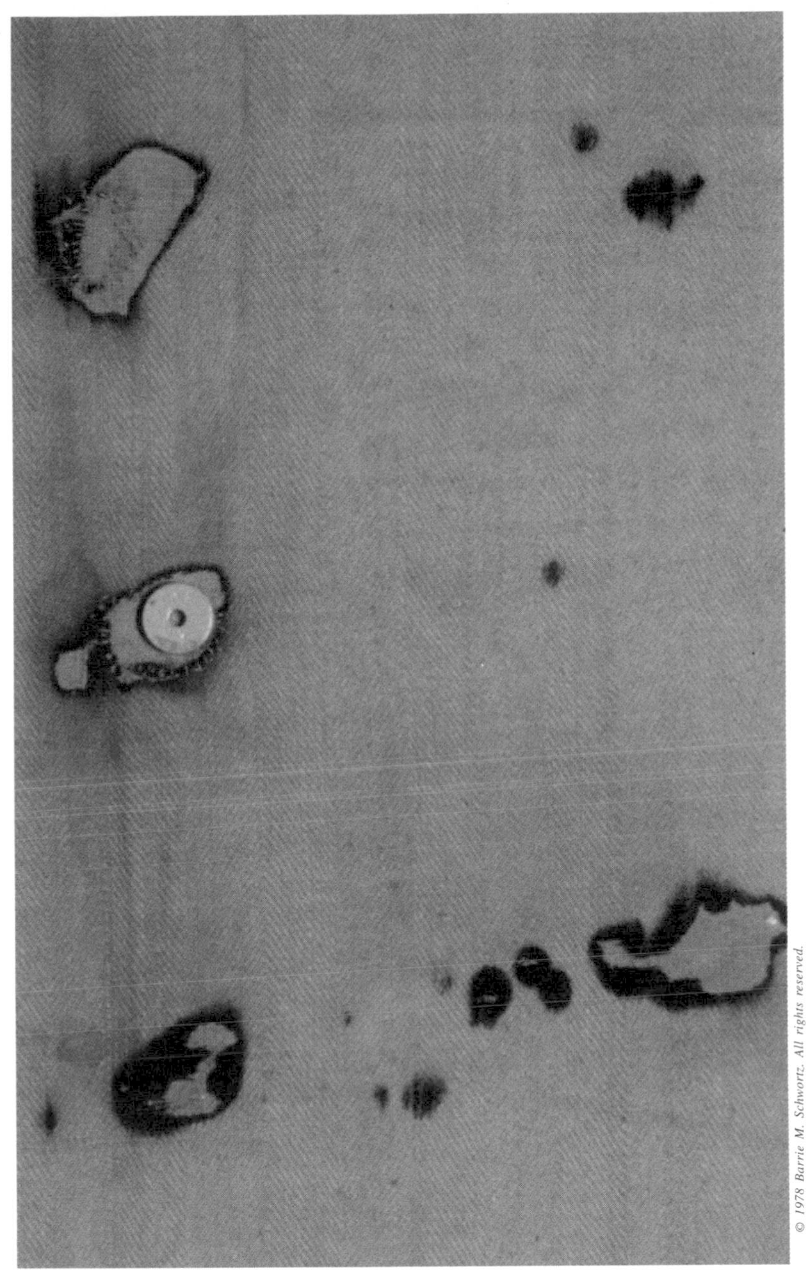



Close-up of poker holes on the actual Shroud.
114-9

Courtesy, Museum of Cluny, Paris.

Pilgrim's Medallion (c. 1355) found in the Seine River. The Medallion depicts the double image of the Shroud and the crests of Geoffrey de Charny and his wife Jeanne de Vergy.

The envelopment of the body of Christ in the Shroud, by Jean Gaspard Baldoino (1590-1669). Painting located in the Chapel of the Holy Shroud, Nice, France.

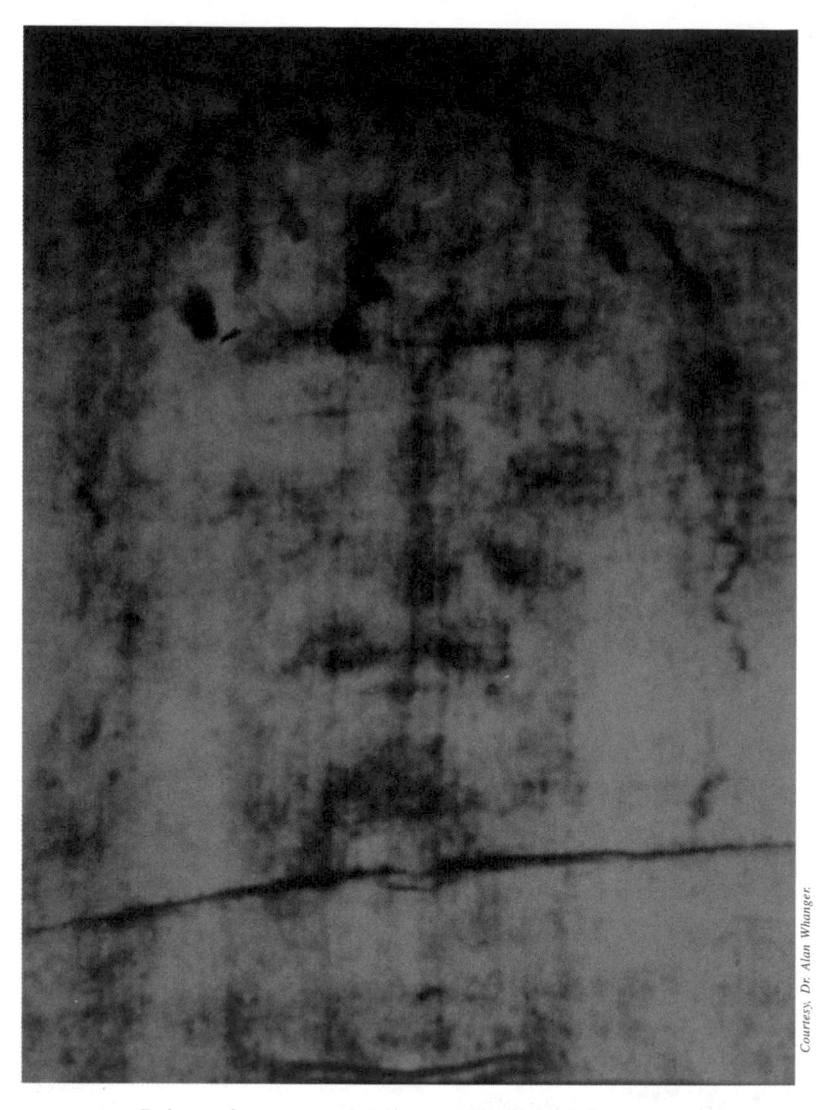

Courtesy, Dr. Alan Whanger.

Points of congruence between the Shroud face and the icon from St. Catherine's Monastery at Mt. Sinai:

1) Hair parted in middle 2) Configuration of hair lines on forehead 3) Configuration of hair lines on side 4) Transverse streak across forehead 5) V shape at bridge of nose 6) Heavily accented owlish eyes 7) Raised right eyebrow 8) Configuration of left eyebrow 9) Right eye larger than left, bulges forward 10) Fold under left eye 11) Fold under right eye 12) Left ear incorporating spots 13) Right ear incorporating spots

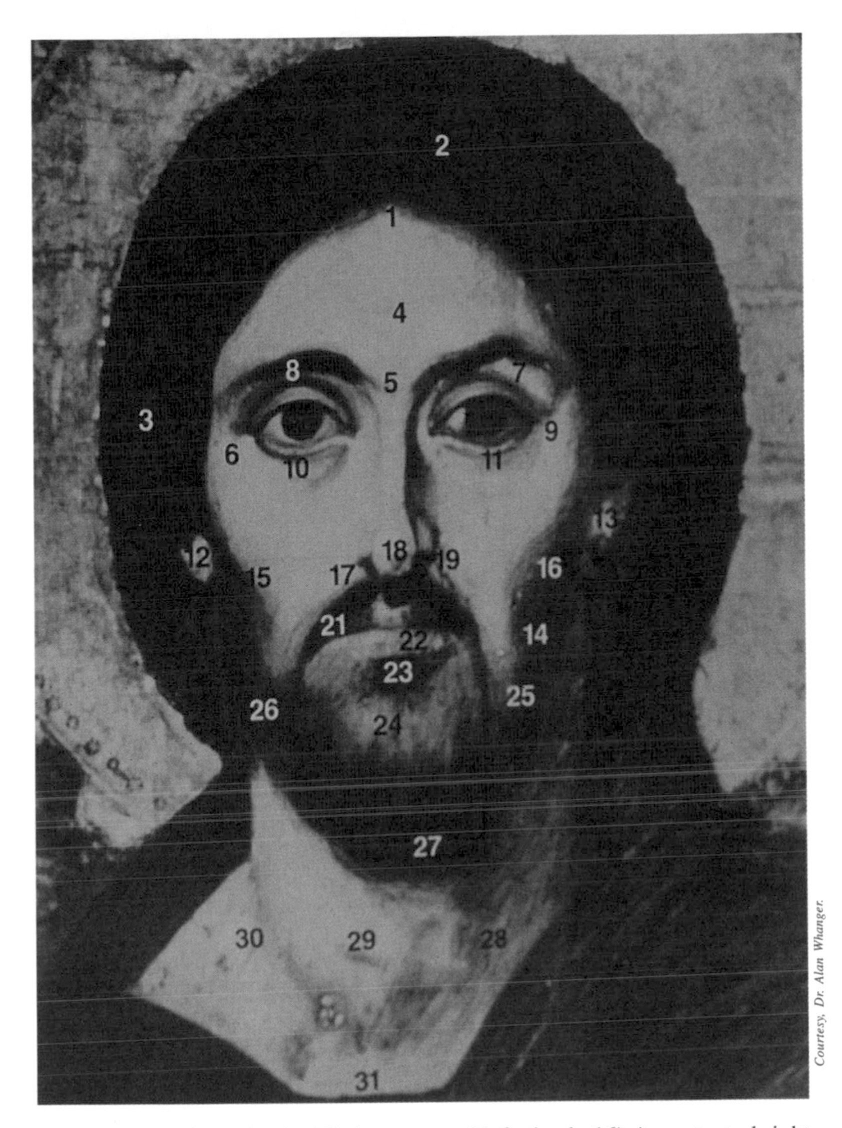


Courtesy, Dr. Alan Whanger.

14) Matter on right cheek 15) Accentuated left cheek 16) Accentuated right cheek 17) Enlarged left nostril 18) Nose tip matches 19) Demarcation of right nostril 20) Accentuated line beneath nose and upper lip 21) Configuration of mustache 22) Configuration of lips 23) Heavy line under lower lip 24) Hairless area between lower lip and beard 25) Margin of beard on right 26) Margin of beard on left 27) Beard configuration 28) Goiter-like folds of right neck 29) Small fold of neck 30) Jagged lines, left neck 31) Transverse line across throat.

114-13

Marks on the Frontal Image:

1. Blood on forehead from crown of thorns.
2. Crease in cloth.
3. Blood from side wound from lance.
4. Water stains from fire of 1532.
5. Nail wound in left wrist.
6. Scorch marks from fire of 1532.
7. Blood from nail wound in foot.

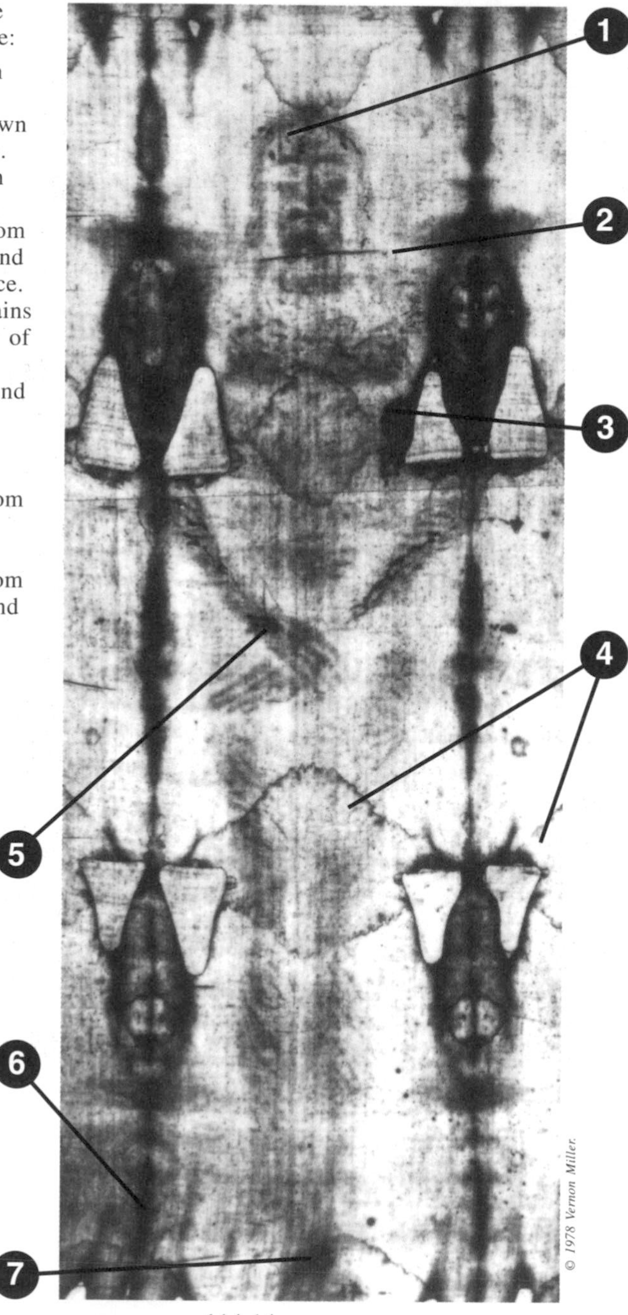

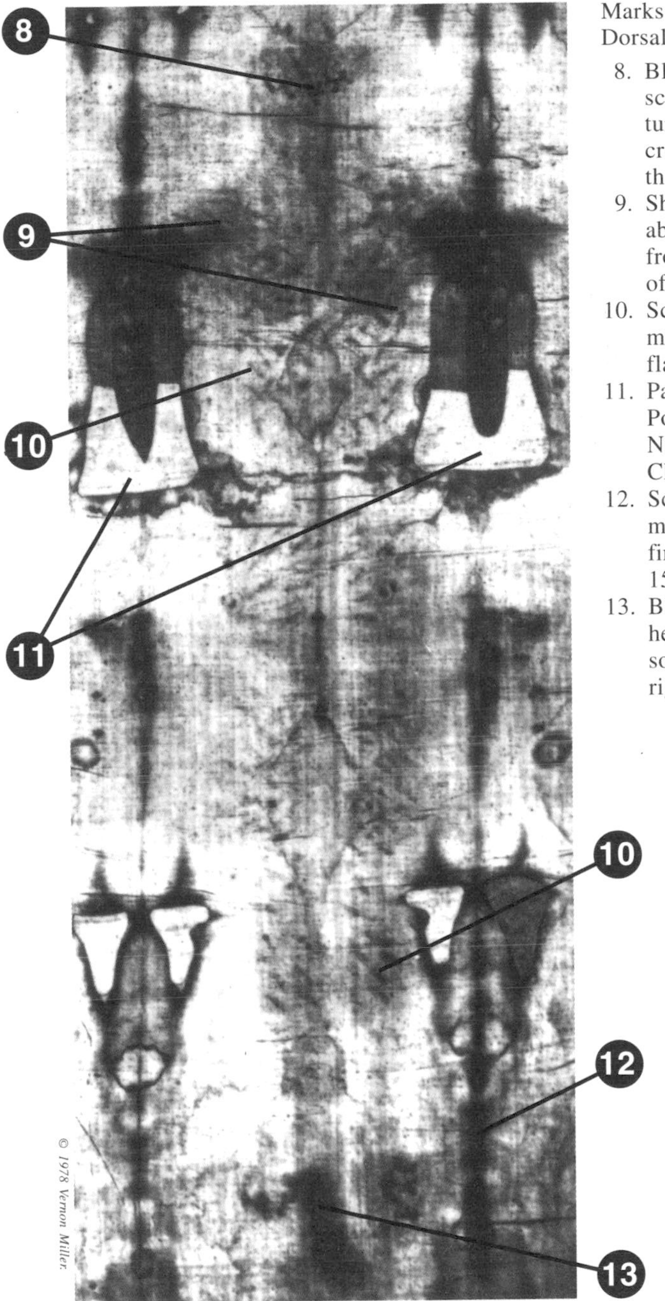




Marks on the Dorsal Image:

8. Blood from scalp punctures due to crown of thorns.
9. Shoulder abrasions from weight of the cross.
10. Scourge marks from flagrum.
11. Patches by Poor Clare Nuns, Chambery.
12. Scorch marks from fire of 1532.
13. Blood from heel and sole of right foot.

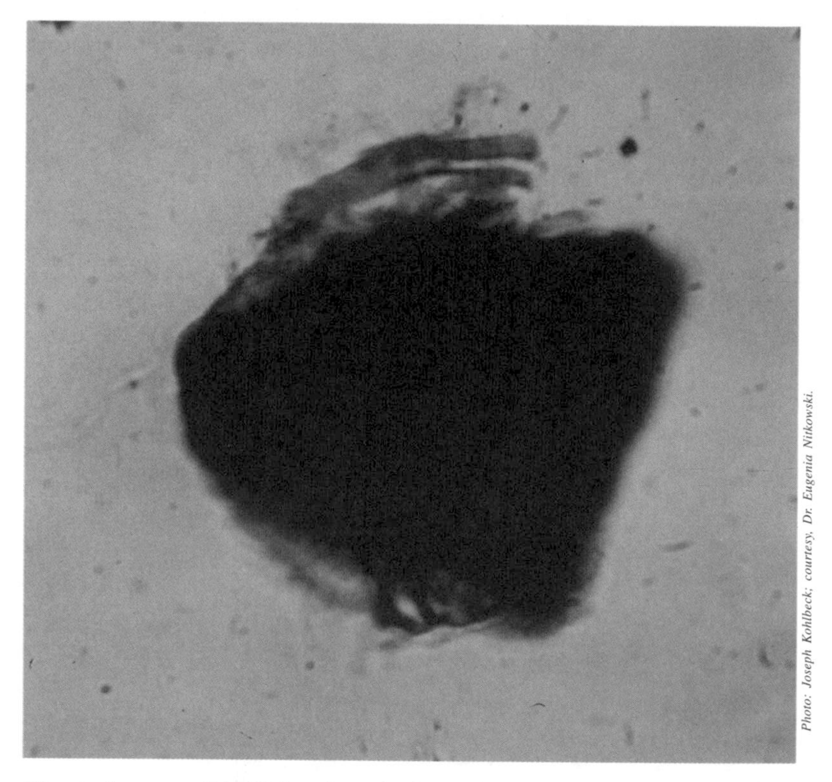

Photo: Joseph Kohlbeck; courtesy, Dr. Eugenia Nitkowski.

Muscle fragment "3BB" found on the lower back of the man on the Shroud.

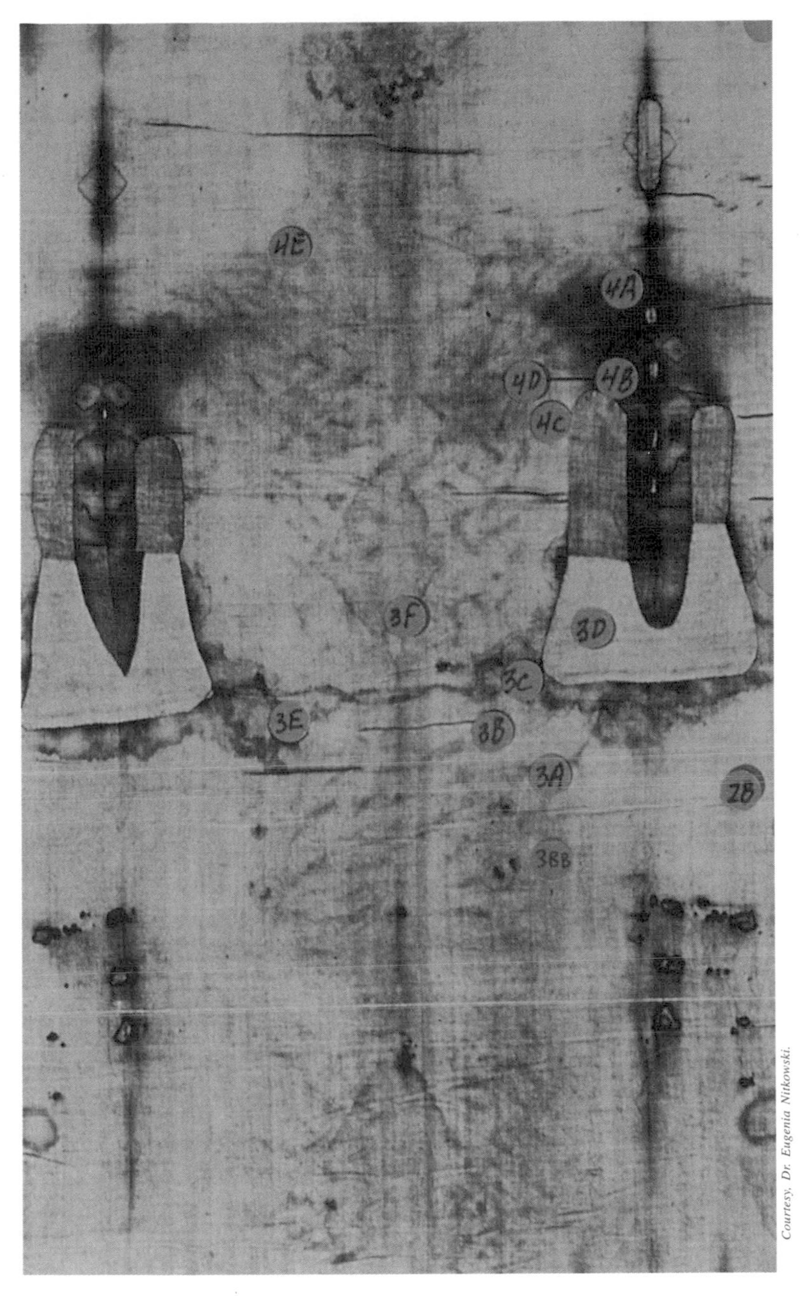


*Courtesy, Dr. Eugenia Nitkowski.*

Location of muscle fragment "3BB."
114-17

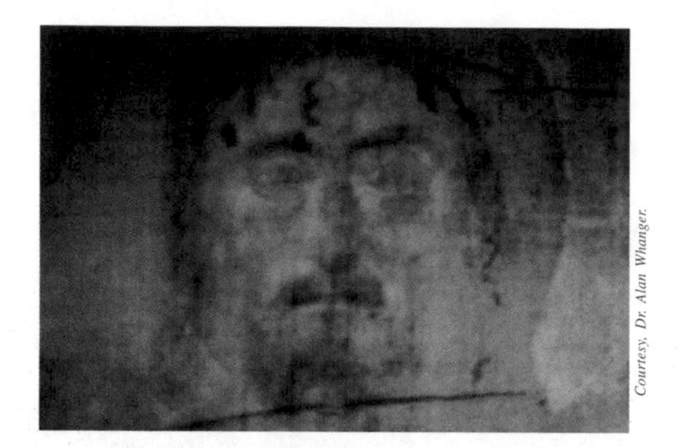

*Courtesy, Dr. Alan Whanger.*

Image of icon at St. Catherine's Monastery superimposed on Shroud face.

*Courtesy, Dr. Alan Whanger.*

The face of Christ on a gold Byzantine coin struck by Emperor Justinian II, dated between 692-695 A.D.

*Courtesy, Dr. Alan Whanger.*

Byzantine coin superimposed on Shroud face to show similarity.

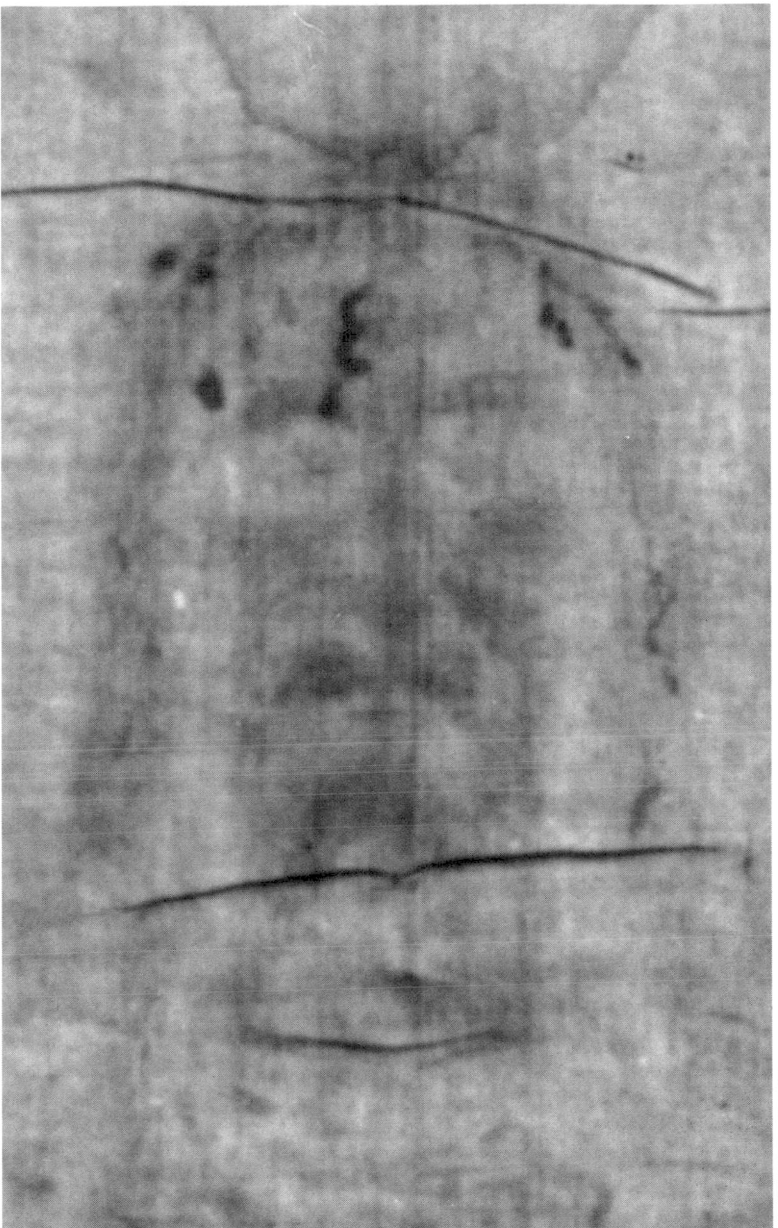



The face of the man on the Shroud as viewed with unaided eye—shown for comparison with images on preceding page.

Pontius Pilate coin depicting astrologer's staff surmounted by letters.

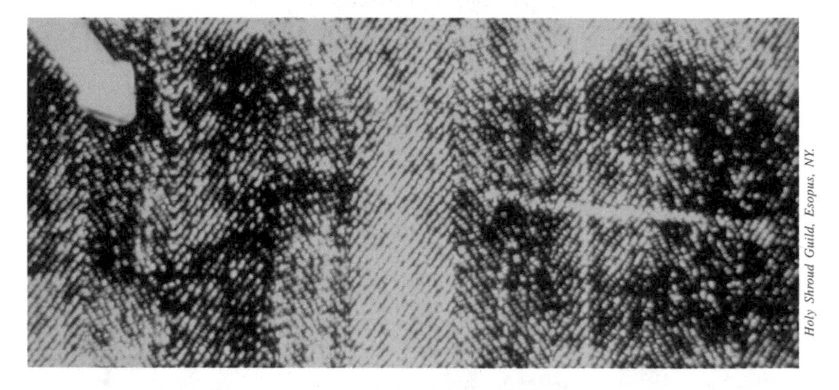


Enrie's photo of Shroud face with arrow pointing to the top of letter "A" on coin over the right eye.

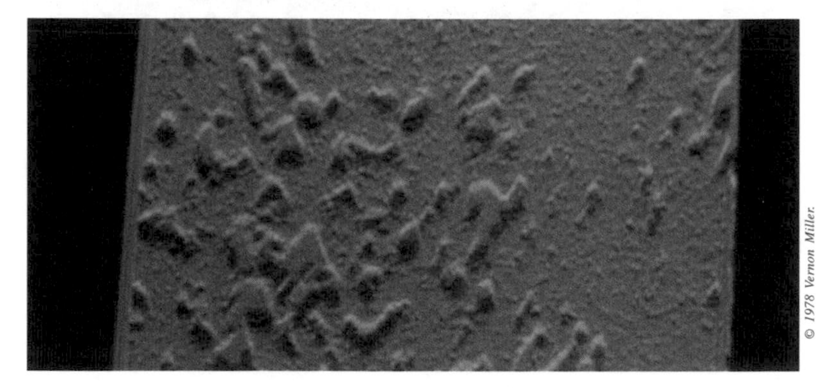


VP8 Image Analyzer image of three-dimensional imprints of coin over right eye. The letters "YCAI" are visible on top left corner.

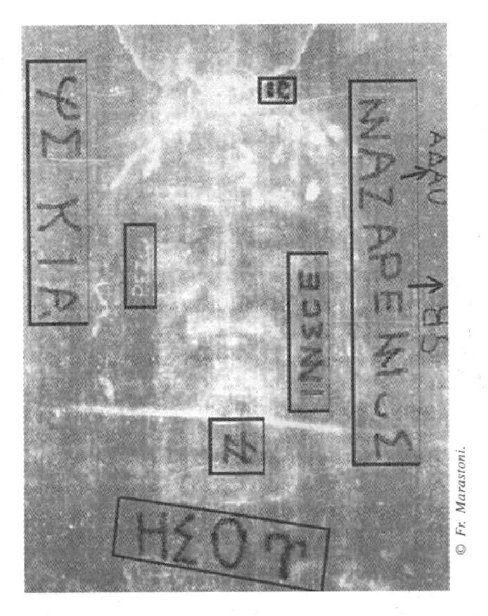



Photographic negative of the Shroud face with supposed Greek inscriptions. Despite the low resolution of this particular photograph, the photo shows where the Greek characters are said to be visible.

Close-up of the herringbone-weave pattern of the Shroud.

Centro Diocesano di Sindonologia, Rome.

Sudarium superimposed over Shroud face. Dr. Alan Whanger found 130 points of congruence between the Sudarium and the Shroud, indicating that the two cloths covered the same face.

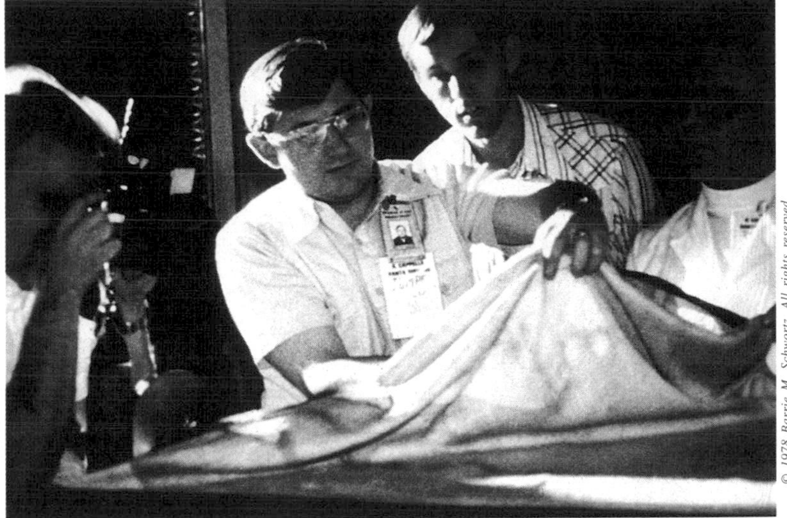



Examination of the Shroud by Dr. John Jackson and Dr. Eric Jumper, U.S. Air Force captains and physicists who headed the STURP Study in 1978. The thirty-plus members of the "Shroud of Turin Research Project," or STURP, brought with them seventy-two crates of equipment and took 30,000 photographs, working around the clock to take advantage of their allotted five days (120 hours). The group was composed of specialists in various disciplines including optical physics, radiography, medicine, botany and photography.

Dr. Max Frei taking pollen samples with sticky tape.
114-24

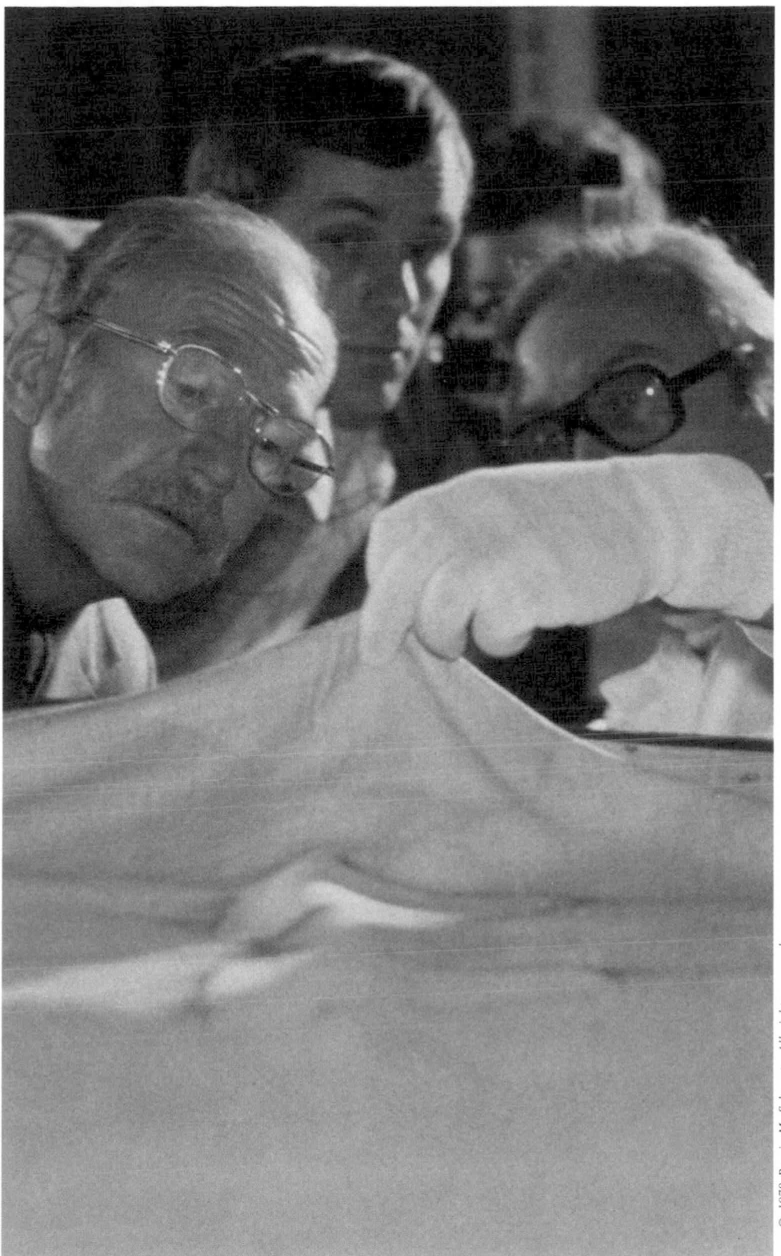


1978 examination of the underside of the Shroud.

114-25

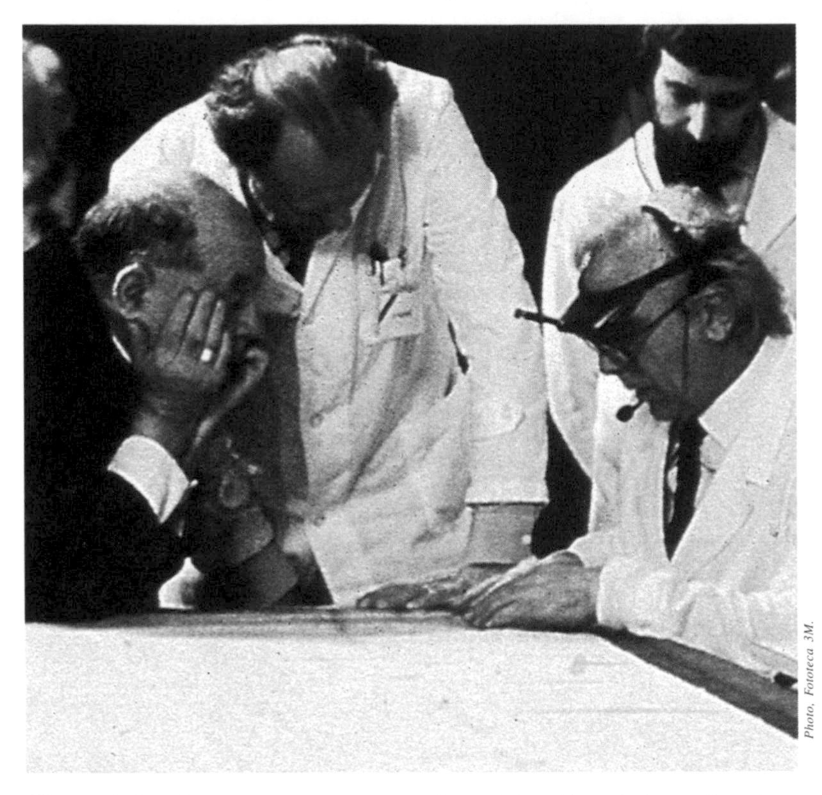

Photo, Fototeca 3M.

Giovanni Riggi preparing to cut samples of the Shroud for radiocarbon dating in 1988. Notice that Riggi is not wearing protective gloves and that Cardinal Ballestrero is leaning on the table.

Photo, Fototeca 3M.

Close-up of the corner where the sample was taken in 1988.

Courtesy, Prof. Douglas Donahue.

The metal tube labeled "A1" designating the Arizona lab. Because the sample was cut inaccurately, this cylinder contained two samples of the Shroud for the radiocarbon dating test in 1988.

*Telegraph Group, Ltd., London.*

Press conference held at the British Museum on October 13, 1988 following the radiocarbon dating. From left to right: Prof. Edward Hall, Dr. Michael Tite and Dr. Robert Hedges.

The Shroud positioned on support table. (Photo from 1978 STURP Study.)

AP/Wide World Photos/Mauro Pilone.

During the night of April 11-12, 1997, a fire broke out in San Giovanni Cathedral in Turin. Here firefighters spray water into the sanctuary of the Guarini chapel, where the Holy Shroud was enshrined.

AP/Wide World Photos/Mauro Pilone.

The glass encasement which contained the silver reliquary of the Holy Shroud lies shattered on the floor of the Cathedral.

Reuters/Claudio Papi/Archive Photos.

Firemen carry the silver reliquary from the burning Turin Cathedral on April 12, 1997.

## Proposals to Test the Shroud Using C-14

Shortly after winning the Nobel Prize for his work in 1961, Libby asked permission to conduct a radiocarbon test on the Shroud. He was refused because the test required the destruction of 870 square centimeters of the cloth. During the studies conducted between 1969 and 1973, the amount of cloth needed for the test was reduced to 500 square centimeters, but no testing was done. Several years later, the sample size was further decreased to 100 square centimeters, but once again the test was not performed.

In 1976, David H. Sox, an Anglican clergyman who was also the secretary of the British Society for the Turin Shroud, was interested in having the Shroud dated. Having heard that Gilbert Raes of the University of Ghent had a sample of the Shroud taken from the 1973 study, Sox, along with McCrone from Chicago, went to Belgium to examine it. They tried to influence Raes to allow the sample to be dated using a technique based on the effect of the disintegration of the radiocarbon atoms on photographic emulsions. Raes was reluctant, and when he informed the diocese of Turin about the matter, he was asked to return the sample, which he did.

A new method of testing called Accelerator Mass Spectrometry (AMS) was devised in 1977 by Harry E. Gove, professor of physics at the University of Rochester, and his colleagues. The advantage of this new technique is that every radioactive carbon atom is included in the reading, not simply the decaying ones. Furthermore, only one-fifth the amount of material was needed for this test, which was considered enough to determine the age of the Shroud to within 150 years.

When Sox heard about this new method, he contacted Gove immediately. Gove, in turn, contacted Robert

Hedges and Edward Hall from Oxford University. Hedges was reluctant while Hall seemed interested. Gove presented this method during the 1978 Second International Congress for the Study of the Shroud held in Turin as being the ideal test to determine the age of the Shroud. But the test was not carried out.

In 1979, Cardinal Ballestrero sent Luigi Gonella, his scientific advisor, to the International Radiocarbon Congress in Heidelberg. Gonella was to consult specialists on the advisability of using the AMS method. At the congress, Gove presented a paper in which he advocated the applicability of this new technique to the Shroud. Gonella then went to meet with Jacques Evin, director of the radiocarbon dating laboratory at the University of Lyons, who advised him against using a method which had not yet been perfected.[2]

On July 15, 1979, Gove, together with Garman Harbottle from the University of Brookhaven, who developed the method of proportional counters which measures radiocarbon by means of small-scale gas counters, sent a proposal to Cardinal Ballestrero. They requested permission to use both methods to test half the sample which Raes had removed from the Shroud back in 1973. Permission was not granted.

In 1982, STURP set up a commission to study the possibility of using the radiocarbon technique to date the Shroud. The commission was headed by Robert Dinegar, a researcher at Los Alamos. He and Gove contacted six laboratories capable of working with small samples. Four of the labs, namely, Rochester, Arizona, Oxford and Zurich made use of the accelerator method. The other two labs at Brookhaven and Harwell made use of the gas counter method.

The 177-page proposal entitled "Phase II" was submitted by D'Muhala and Jackson to Cardinal Ballestrero on October 16, 1984. The proposal was based on the findings of Gove and Harbottle with some modifications. They suggested that six samples be taken from different parts of the Shroud which would then be distributed by STURP, who would act as the "submitter" to the six laboratories. Cardinal Ballestrero promised to send the proposal to the Holy See.

Another proposal for a C-14 test was submitted to the Cardinal in May 1985 by William Meacham, an American archaeologist living in Hong Kong. He suggested that the following five samples be taken from the Shroud:

1) a single thread from the middle of the cloth between the dorsal and ventral images,
2) a small piece cut just in from the edge next to the site of Raes' piece I,
3) a piece of the charred cloth,
4) a piece cut from the side strip next to the site of Raes' II,
5) a piece of the backing cloth sewn on in 1534.[3]

In Meacham's view, such a test would produce two or three radiocarbon ages that would agree with one another, thereby giving a reliable date for the calendar age of the linen Shroud.

## Trondheim Protocol

In June 1985, at the International Congress of Radiocarbon Dating held in Trondheim, Norway, Gove proposed to the representatives of the other five laboratories that they separate from STURP and continue on their own. His reason was that they would be able to carry out the tests themselves and not have to rely on STURP which had to commission others for the tests. The labs agreed. They proposed the following protocol which was put forth as being an honest and wise implementation of the STURP project:

1) The British Museum would be the co-ordinating body and the "guarantor" of the investigations.
2) The "good services" of STURP would be requested to organize the cutting operation.
3) The British Museum would supply two additional samples of known dates with a difference of at least ± 150 years. The three samples, including that of the Shroud, would be unravelled and the threads cut up to render them as indistinguishable as possible.
4) The British Museum would obtain a written declaration from the laboratories not to divulge the results to anybody, except those authorized and designated by the Museum.
5) The six laboratories could use any method of their choice to prepare the specimens for dating, but detailed descriptions should be carefully recorded of the procedure and the manner in which their average values and their uncertainties were assessed.
6) The results would be sent to the Holy See and the Archbishop of Turin before publication.[4]

An uproar immediately ensued after this proposal was made. Dinegar, who was present at the Trondheim Congress, insisted that the radiocarbon dating was only one of the tests which was part of the STURP project and that it should not have priority over the others. He believed that the radiocarbon testing should only be done after the analysis of the fiber contents which was the domain of Heller and Adler. Gove announced he would drop everything if STURP were allowed to do anything other than cut the samples. Sox regretted that they were even allowed to do as much. Giovanni Riggi stated: "The Carbon-14 war was declared against our group by Professor Gove, without any possibility of coming to an agreement."[5]

## Turin Protocol

At this time, Cardinal Ballestrero called for a preparatory meeting of scientists and researchers at the major seminary in Turin from September 29 to October 1, 1986. The twenty-six participants included Professor Carlos Chagas, president of the Pontifical Academy of Sciences; his secretary, Vittorio Canuto, an astrophysicist at the NASA Institute for Space Studies in New York; representatives from the six laboratories, with Jean-Claude Duplessy from Gif-sur-Yvette in France, a seventh laboratory; Mechtilde Flury-Lemberg, a textile expert from Berne, who was invited by Chagas; Gove and his secretary, Shirley Brignall; Paul Damon and Douglas Donahue from the Tucson laboratory; Edward Hall and Robert Hedges from Oxford; and Willy Wölfli, director of the lab at Zurich Polytechnic. Also present were Dr. Adler and Dinegar representing STURP, Gonella, Riggi, Evin, Tite, Meacham and a few others.

The protocol called for a "double blind" analysis of three samples: one from the Shroud and two control samples supplied by the British Museum. Each of these would be given to the seven laboratories who were not to share any information with one another. Five of the labs would use the AMS method to date the samples, and the other two would use the small counters. The specimens were not to be cut from any burnt area of the Shroud. The person selected to cut the samples was

Mechtilde Flury-Lemberg. When the tests were completed, a date would be set to submit the results to three institutions for analysis, namely, the Pontifical Academy of Sciences, the British Museum and the G. Colonnetti Institute of Metrology of Turin.

Such was the plan until April 27, 1987, when Gonella reported to the newspaper *La Stampa* that only two or three labs would be conducting the tests. Surprised by this unforeseen turn of events, Gove encouraged the seven laboratories to send telegrams to Cardinal Ballestrero as well as to the Vatican protesting this breach of protocol. The Cardinal then sent a letter to all the labs on October 10, 1987, informing them of the Holy See's instructions on how to proceed. Three laboratories were chosen to carbon date the Shroud. The labs selected were Arizona, Oxford and Zurich, all of which use the accelerator method. One of the labs that was dropped was Harwell, which had more experience than the six labs combined. Even Gove remarked: "Harwell probably can obtain the most accurate dating of all of us."[6] Hall of Oxford also felt that "Harwell would have been a good addition."[7] Interestingly, the Pontifical Academy of Sciences was also eliminated as one of the coordinating and guaranteeing institutions. However, Professor Chagas, from the aforementioned Academy, was invited as a guest of the Cardinal to witness the cutting of the samples which would no longer be done by Mechtilde Flury-Lemberg, but by Riggi. Tite from the British Museum would be the sole guarantor.

In December 1987, the directors of the three laboratories sent a letter to Cardinal Ballestrero indicating their preference for the original Turin protocol. They pointed out that "there are many critics in the world who will scrutinize these measurements in great detail. The abandonment of the original protocol and the decision to proceed with only three laboratories will certainly enhance the skepticism of these critics."[8]

On January 15, 1988, Gove and Harbottle held a press conference at Columbia University in New York to publicly express their disagreement with the decision of using only three laboratories. Dr. Damon from the Arizona lab also argued that "when you're doing research, you always have that thing that doesn't fit: 'What did we do wrong? Could we have mixed the samples? Was there an error in the lab?' You can't do that with something like the shroud. You've got to get it right the first time. I would prefer seven labs to three for a number of reasons. . . ."[9] Gove complained that "Gonella is simply the wrong man. . . . a second-rate scientist . . . a man nobody has ever heard of . . . I wish I knew how he got to be scientific advisor."[10]

Gonella responded to the charges of his critics by stating that the reduction in the number of laboratories used would minimize the amount of damage to the Shroud. He further added: "There was no scientific reason to make use of seven laboratories. Having a good number to carry out the test would in no way change the amount of uncertainty. Even if we were to use fifty laboratories."[11] Gove countered by saying that the amount of cloth needed for the tests was insignificant to justify the exclusion of four laboratories. As an illustration, he said that if the Shroud were covered with 8,800 twenty-two cent stamps, the amount needed by the seven labs would equal two and one-half stamps.[12]

On January 22, 1988, Tite, Gonella and the three representatives from the labs met at the British Museum. Wilson and Tite listened to Gonella complain about Gove. Robert Otlet, a radiocarbon expert, said that he believed the real problem was Gonella's dislike for Gove. If Gonella were to change the procedure at this juncture, it would give the impression he was acquiescing to Gove.[13] During this meeting the protocol to be used was drawn up and subsequently publicized in a letter by Tite in the journal *Nature*:

> Following my letter of 11 June 1987 . . . I am now able to provide an outline of the procedures that have been finally agreed for the radiocarbon dating of the Shroud of Turin. Of the seven original offers to undertake the dating of the Shroud, three have been accepted by Cardinal Ballestrero, Archbishop of Turin and Pontifical Custodian of the Shroud. The radiocarbon laboratories concerned are at the University of Arizona, the University of Oxford and the Federal Institute of Technology in Zurich, and each has now agreed to proceed with the project.
>
> Each laboratory will be provided with a sample from the shroud, together with two known-age control samples, one of which will have been independently dated by conventional radiocarbon dating. The shroud samples will be taken from a single site on the main body of the shroud away from any patches or charred areas. In order to ensure that ample carbon for dating survives after pretreatment, the weight of each cloth sample (that is, shroud and controls) will be 40 mg. All the samples will be given to the laboratories as whole pieces of cloth without being unravelled or shredded. A blind test procedure will be adopted in that the three samples given to each laboratory will be labelled 1, 2, and 3 and the laboratories will not be told which sample comes from the shroud. Even if the samples were shredded, it would still be possible for a laboratory to distinguish the shroud sample from the others. It is therefore accepted that the blind test depends ultimately on the good faith of the laboratories.

> The removal of the samples from the shroud will be undertaken under the supervision of a qualified textile expert. These samples will be weighed, wrapped in aluminum foil and sealed in numbered stainless steel containers. The control samples will be similarly treated. All these operations will be watched over and certified by Cardinal Ballestrero in collaboration with myself. After they have been packaged, we will immediately hand over three samples (shroud and two controls) to representatives of each of the three radiocarbon dating laboratories who will be in Turin for this purpose. In addition, all stages will be fully documented by video film and photography.
>
> On completion of their measurements, the laboratories will send their data for the three samples to both myself at the British Museum and to the Institute of Metrology "G. Colonnetti" in Turin for preliminary statistical analysis. The laboratories have agreed not to discuss their results with each other until after they have deposited their data for statistical analysis. A final discussion of the measurement data will be made at a subsequent meeting in Turin between representatives of these two institutions and representatives of the three laboratories at which the identity of the three samples will be revealed. The results as finalized at this meeting will form a basis for both a scientific paper and for communication to the public. The timetable for the operations has not yet been fully established but it is hoped that a radiocarbon date for the Shroud of Turin will be released by the end of 1988.[14]

Gove rebutted Tite in an open letter to the same publication by stating:

> The involvement of seven laboratories has been reduced to three. This eliminates the possibility of detecting a mistake made in the measurement by one or more of the three laboratories. As Tite knows, such mistakes are not unusual.
>
> The use of both decay counting and accelerator mass spectrometry (AMS) has been changed to AMS only. The two methods are distinct and independent.
>
> The amount of cloth each AMS laboratory receives has been increased by almost a factor of two. With this much material, several more laboratories could have been included . . .
>
> The scientific body connected with the Roman Catholic Church which has a high reputation in the world of science, the Pontifical Academy of Sciences, has unaccountably been excluded from official participation in any aspect of this important and controversial radiocarbon measurement.
>
> The acknowledged textile expert selected at the Turin Workshop to remove the Shroud sample has been replaced by some unnamed person.
>
> All these unnecessary and unexplained changes unilaterally dictated by the Archbishop of Turin will produce an age for the Turin Shroud which will be vastly less credible than that which could have been obtained if the original Turin Workshop protocol had been followed. Perhaps that is just what the Turin authorities intend.[15]

Gove implies that the Cardinal deliberately approved a questionable procedure in order to "save face" should the tests reveal a medieval age for the Shroud. This feeling was shared by others including Harbottle: "The church has scaled down some of the precautions planned to ensure credibility of the test results. Professor Gove and I have deep reservations about this. We're concerned that we may be opening the door to enormous controversy and endless, endless bickering and recriminations that could go on and on . . . With only three pieces of data, the project is fraught with danger."[16]

## Cutting of the Samples

In the early morning hours of April 21, 1988, the triple-lock silver reliquary containing the Shroud was removed unceremoniously from its place in the Guarini Chapel and brought into the sacristy of the cathedral. There it was placed on a table covered with aluminum foil and unfolded by Monsignor Pietro Caramello and another priest wearing gloves. Those involved in the project numbered more than thirty. Among those present were Riggi; Cardinal Ballestrero, accompanied by five priests (including Caramello); Gonella; Monsignor Dardozzi, who was a representative from the Pontifical Academy of Sciences; Tite; Franco Testore and Gabriel Vial (both textile experts); and representatives from the three labs—Hall and Hedges from Oxford, Damon and Donahue from Tucson, and Wölfli from Zurich.

When the Cardinal asked the textile experts the place from which the samples were to be taken, neither one had any idea because of their limited knowledge of the Shroud. It is said that when Testore saw the stain of the side wound on the cloth he asked: "What's that large brown patch?"[17] After discussing the matter for over an hour, Riggi cut a single piece, without wearing gloves, from the same corner where Raes had taken his sample in 1973.[18] This spot is often referred to as "Raes' corner" and is located on the bottom right of the frontal image. The sample site chosen was not ideal as it was along the side strip, only a few centimeters away from burn marks caused by the molten silver from the fire of 1532, and was most likely a contaminated source.[19]

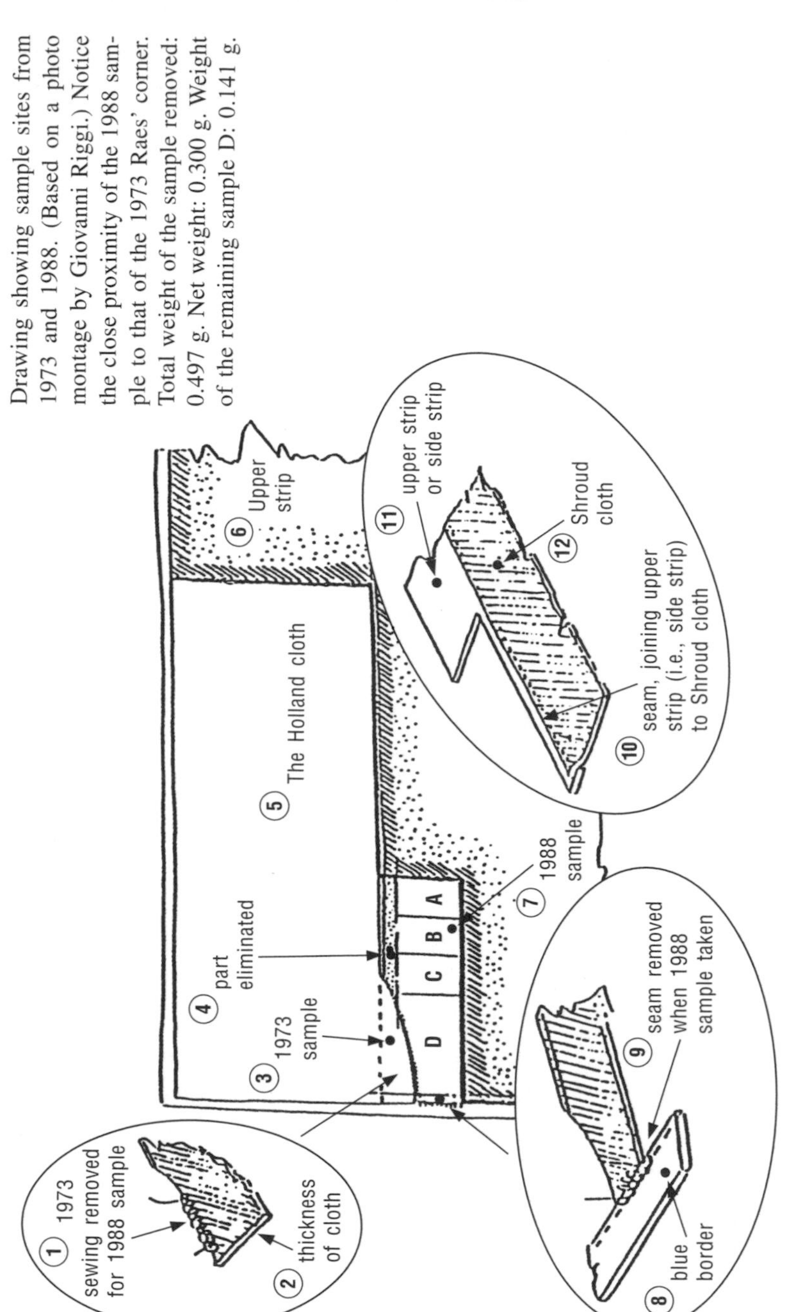


Drawing showing sample sites from 1973 and 1988. (Based on a photo montage by Giovanni Riggi.) Notice the close proximity of the 1988 sample to that of the 1973 Raes' corner. Total weight of the sample removed: 0.497 g. Net weight: 0.300 g. Weight of the remaining sample D: 0.141 g.

Professor Hall denied this in an interview, saying: "the sample was *not* taken from the edge; nor, incidentally, was the piece taken by Professor Raes."[20] A photo of the sample being cut clearly shows that the specimen was near a repair site. Dr. Adler remarked that "the sample used for dating . . . came from an area that is water-stained and scorched, and the edge is back-woven, indicating repair."[21] Upon closer examination one notices the weave pattern of this patch cloth is "S" twist whereas the Shroud weave is "Z" twist. The Whangers also maintained that "an X-ray of that sample area of the Shroud reveals the presence of additional threads extending from the seam into the fabric to a distance of about an inch and one-half, more than far enough to cross the entire width of the sample removed."[22]

According to the official report, a strip measuring 10 mm x 70 mm was cut from which three pieces weighing approximately 50 mg each were made.[23] However, Riggi admits the strip was actually 81 mm x 16 mm.[24] He relates that the sample size was further reduced because there were "threads of another type which, even in a minimal quantity, could have brought about variations in the dating, since they were later additions."[25] The original sample sizes were of unequal weight: 52 mg, 52.8 mg and 39.6 mg, so Riggi had to add another piece of 14.1 mg to the latter to bring its weight up to 53.7 mg.[26] This means that one of the laboratories received a tube containing two pieces of the Shroud. Riggi then proceeded to cut three additional pieces from each of the two samples brought by Tite, which would serve as control samples. The first linen sample, dated between the eleventh and twelfth centuries A.D., was from a Nubian tomb. The second sample, dated from the early second century A.D., came from a Theban mummy. Both samples were provided by the British Museum.

The entire proceeding was done in full view of the scientists and cameras except for the one-half hour when the samples were taken into a side room by Cardinal Ballestrero and Dr. Tite. It has been reported, however, that Gonella and Riggi were also present for this procedure.[27] There the samples were wrapped in aluminum foil and placed into nine stainless steel containers and sealed with the red seal wax of the Cardinal. The Shroud sample was placed in the tube labeled number one. The containers for Zurich were marked Z1, Z2, and Z3; the ones for Oxford were labeled O1, O2, and O3; and the ones for Arizona were A1 (which had two pieces of the Shroud), A2, and A3.

Contrary to the protocol letter drafted by Tite regarding the anonymity of the samples, a letter signed by the Cardinal and Tite was given to each of the three laboratories along with their samples. Each letter was similar in content to the one below given to the Zurich lab:

> The containers labelled Z1, Z2, and Z3 to be delivered to representatives of ETH contain one sample of cloth taken in our presence from the Shroud of Turin at 9:45 am, 21 April 1988, and two control samples from one or both of the following cloths supplied by the British Museum: First-century cloth; eleventh century. The identity of the samples put in the individual containers has been recorded by a special notebook that will be kept confidential until the measurements have been made.[28]

Even though the labs were not told which tube contained the Shroud sample, the fact that this information was made known violates the objective purpose of having control samples. Furthermore, "because the distinctive three-to-one herringbone twill weave of the shroud could not be matched in the controls . . . it was possible for a laboratory to identify the shroud sample."[29] Wölfli himself admitted: "All you would need is to look at the pictures in the *National Geographic Magazine*. It didn't take me long to know. It is Z1."[30]

## The Fourth Sample

In February 1988, Dr. Tite asked Evin for a sample of medieval linen, preferably from the fourteenth century, having the same color and weave of the Shroud. Evin attempted to obtain such a sample from the Museum of Cluny but was refused because they were unwilling to cut six centimeters from any of their artifacts. Undaunted, Evin then went to Saint-Maximin-la-Sainte-Baume in Provence, where he was able to obtain a sample of threads from the cope of St. Louis of Anjou (1274-1297).

For reasons unknown, Tite was unable to go to France to obtain the sample, so he asked that Evin mail it to him. But fearing postal strikes, not uncommon in Europe, Evin had the sample hand delivered to Tite by Gabriel Vial from the *Musee Historique des Tissus* in Lyons on the morning of April 21.

Shortly after all the samples were sealed in their respective cylinders, either Evin or Vial took out the cope sample. This caught Riggi by surprise as he had no knowledge of this extra sample. By this time Cardinal Ballestrero had left. Gonella and Tite insisted that this other control sample be included, given all the trouble Evin had gone through to get it. As there were no other stainless steel containers prepared for this fourth sample, the threads were placed in envelopes, contrary to Evin's report that there were four metal containers.[31]

The official report states: "the three containers containing the shroud . . . and two control samples . . . were then handed to representatives of each of the three laboratories together with a sample of a third control . . . which was in the form of threads."[32]

Later in the evening of April 21, the scientists departed for their own labs in their respective countries to conduct their tests.

## Preliminary Test Preparations

Before the samples were tested, they were first cleaned using chemical and mechanical methods: "Each was thoroughly cleaned and burned to produce carbon dioxide and then pure carbon, whose atoms were electrified. A high-energy mass spectrometer separated the carbon isotopes and counted their atoms. From their ratio came the fabric's age."[33]

The laboratory in Zurich divided each sample in half, each of which was further subdivided into three. One third received no additional treatment, one third was treated with a weak solution of .05% hydrochloric acid, followed by 0.25% sodium hydroxide, followed again by 0.5% hydrochloric acid at room temperature with intermittent washings. The last third was treated with a strong solution of 5% hydrochloric acid, then by 2.5% sodium hydroxide, which was followed again with 5% hydrochloric acid at temperatures of 80°C and intermittent washings.

The laboratory in Arizona divided each sample into four sub-samples. One pair was treated with diluted hydrochloric acid, diluted sodium hydroxide, and again with hydrochloric acid with intermittent washings. The other pair was cleaned with commercial detergents, hydrochloric acid, ethanol, and distilled water.

The laboratory in Oxford divided the samples into three. Each was treated with hydrochloric acid, sodium hydroxide, and again with hydrochloric acid at a temperature of 80°C with intermittent washings. Two of the three pieces were also bleached in sodium hypochlorite.[34]

## Test Results

The first lab to report its results to Tite was the Tucson laboratory on May 6, 1988. The second lab to submit its data was Zurich on May 26. Finally, Oxford submitted its results several months later on August 8, more than ample time to hear of the results of the other two labs. Subsequently, the journal *Nature* reported that "the results of radiocarbon measurements in Arizona, Oxford and Zurich yield a calibrated calendar age range with at least 95% confidence for the linen of the Shroud of Turin of A.D. 1260-1390. . . . These results therefore provide conclusive evidence that the linen of the Shroud of Turin is mediaeval."[35]

Even before the data was officially reported to the proper Church authorities, there were leaks in the media. Sox, who was privy to the tests in Zurich, anticipated the publication of the results by producing a program for the BBC which aired on July 27, 1988. The program, originally entitled *Verdict on the Shroud*, was surreptitiously renamed *Threads of Evidence* when the results were not forthcoming.

The following month, on August 26, the headline for London's *Evening Standard* was "The Shroud of Turin is a Fake." When rumors of forgery reached Turin, it provoked the ire of Gonella. He complained, "If any researcher has spoken, it means that he took the trouble to verify which of the three samples delivered to each of the three laboratories came from the Shroud.

We had trusted them; now we are disillusioned."[36] Contrary to Tite's protocol letter which stated the labs would not communicate with one another, he acknowledged that the "results from each testing centre have been circulated to the others with a proposal for a coordinated date on the Shroud from the samples. . . ."[37] Years later it was reported that the Arizona laboratory had produced eight different measurements rather than the four mentioned in the *Nature* report.[38]

While news of the Shroud's alleged medieval origin was spreading like wildfire, people were beginning to wonder why the Church remained silent. Some interpreted the Church's seemingly noncommittal stance as her reticence to accept the verdict of science. Nothing could be further from the truth. The Church has always held science in esteem. Little is it known that it was Pope Clement VIII who established the Pontifical Academy of Sciences in 1603. The reason for the Church's apparent silence was that Cardinal Ballestrero, the Pontifical Custodian of the Shroud, and the Holy See had not been informed. It was not until September 28, 1988 that Tite conveyed the test results to the Cardinal who, in turn, relayed the information to the Vatican the following day. Two weeks later Prof. Chagas resigned as President of the Pontifical Academy of Sciences.

The actual scientific report was not submitted to Church officials until one month after the British Museum issued a letter to the Cardinal informing him of the conclusion of a medieval date of the Shroud. The press release and the scientific report were to have been released simultaneously. Gonella expressed his consternation by saying: "I find it inconceivable that today, a month after the official communication of the radiocarbon investigation, we still have to wait for the publication of the entire report regarding the work and the comprehensive evaluation of the laboratories."[39]

The report by the 21 scientists was finally made public in the journal *Nature*, February 16, 1989, five months after the announcement of the test results was made. Standard scientific procedures call for a critique of the data through peer review; this was not followed in this case.

On October 14, 1988, the day after Cardinal Ballestrero issued his press release, the British Museum held its own press conference. Seated at table were Tite flanked by Hedges and Hall. Behind them on a blackboard was written the estimated date: "1260-1390!" The non-professional addition of the exclamation mark is an indication of their unrestrained jubilation over the results.

## Breaches of Protocol and Evidence of Partiality

There is other ample evidence that the C-14 test was fraught with breaches of protocol. For example, two outsiders were present at the labs, namely, Gove in Tucson and Sox in Zurich. When Cardinal Ballestrero learned of this, he strongly objected.

Initially, the Cardinal seemed to accept the test result, but in an interview years later said: "In my opinion, the Turin Shroud is authentic. The radiocarbon measurements, dating the Shroud in the Middle Ages, would appear to have been performed without due care."[40]

It was well known that Gove and Sox were not favorably disposed toward the probable authenticity of the Shroud. Professor Gove admitted in his book: "I had a bet with Shirley [his secretary] on the shroud's age—she bet 2000 $\pm$ 100 years old and I bet 1000 $\pm$ 100 years. Whoever won bought the other a pair of cowboy boots."[41] Wölfli was quoted in an interview as saying: "Knowing the shroud's history, I didn't believe it was two thousand years old, and the test confirmed my opinion."[42] Sox had his negative book on the Shroud published two weeks in advance of the official scientific publication and vehemently denounced the idea of himself taking "the entire blame" for any leaks.[43]

Another individual who seems to have been eager to profit from the Shroud verdict was Hall. A major British newspaper reported that he had planned to obtain a large grant for his laboratory by selling his story of the test results to a Sunday newspaper.[44] When questioned about press leaks, Hall replied: "So it was 'leaked' by the press . . . in the States long before the newspaper stories started here. . . . Everyone was resigned to it being a fake long before the announcement. In this sense it was out of the bag from the very beginning."[45] It was alleged that he received at least £100,000 from ITV for notifying them of the C-14 dating prior to its official pronouncement.[46] On Good Friday, March 25, 1989, 45 businessmen and influential people had given Hall £1 million as a token of appreciation for his work and particularly for establishing that the Shroud was a medieval forgery.[47] Hall used the money to create a new chair of archaeological science and was succeeded later that year by none other than Dr. Tite. In an unexpected letter to Gonella dated September 14, 1989, Tite declared: "I am writing to put on record the fact that I myself do *not* consider that the result of the radiocarbon dating of the Turin Shroud shows the Shroud to be a forgery. . . . I myself have always carefully tried to avoid using the word forgery in discussing the radiocarbon dating of the Shroud."[48]

## Unreliability of Carbon-14 Testing

Commenting on data-collecting for Carbon-14 testing, Dr. Nitowski remarked, "In any form of inquiry or scientific discipline, it is the weight of evidence which must be considered conclusive. In archaeology, if there are ten lines of evidence, carbon-dating being one of them, and it conflicts with the other nine, there is little hesitation to throw out the carbon date as inaccurate due to unforeseen contamination."[49] With regard to the Shroud of Turin, the Carbon-14 test was the only one that did not agree with other data—which support the authenticity of the cloth.

Meacham reiterated the same sentiments at a symposium on the Shroud held in Hong Kong in March 1986:

> There appears to be an unhealthy consensus approaching the level of dogma among both scientific and lay commentators, that C-14 will "settle the issue once and for all time." This attitude sharply contradicts the general perspective of field archaeologists and geologists, who view possible contamination as a very serious problem in interpreting the results of radiocarbon measurement. . . . I find little awareness of the limitations of the C-14 method, an urge to "date first and ask questions later," and a general disregard for the close collaboration between field and laboratory personnel which is the ideal in archaeometric projects. . . . Among specialists who frequently make use of the test, it is not considered as a method which produces an "absolute date" for every sample that can be measured. . . . I doubt that anyone with significant experience in dating . . . samples would dismiss for one moment the potential danger of contamination and other sources of error. No responsible field archaeologist would

> trust a single date, or a series of dates on a single feature, to settle a major historical issue. . . . No responsible radiocarbon scientist would claim that it was proven that all contaminants had been removed and that the dating range produced for a sample was without doubt its actual age.[50]

There are two requirements needed to determine the reliability of radiocarbon testing: the first is the uniform distribution of Carbon-14 in the atmosphere, and the second involves the atmospheric origin of the carbon found in living organisms. Libby's theory is premised upon the constancy of the relation between C-14 and C-12 in the atmosphere. Science cannot, however, confirm this constancy for the past thousands of years. Various factors can affect this relationship, such as the natural magnetism of the earth, the amounts of carbonic anhydride and water vapor in the atmosphere, volcanic eruptions, forest fires and industrial pollutants. With regard to the Shroud, in its long history it has been subjected to fire, water, handling, incense, candle smoke (as is evident from wax drippings), humidity, pollution and any number of other contaminants. Libby himself suggests that 10-15% of the Shroud's weight is made up of foreign organic matter;[51] this would skew the results of a C-14 test.

As early as 1982, a secret test was conducted on a single thread from the Shroud which had been given to scientists at the University of California to be radiocarbon dated. The results showed one end of the thread to be from 200 A.D., and the other end from 1000 A.D.[52] The discrepancy was said to be due to the presence of starch. Given that this was an unauthorized test, the results were never taken into account.

In 1983, Evin had cautioned that the AMS method was not infallible. Studies conducted in May of that same year with the six labs interested in dating the Shroud showed how unreliable C-14 testing really is. The British Museum arranged for each of the laboratories to receive two samples for testing. One sample was flax from Egypt dating back to 3000 B.C., and the other was Peruvian cotton from 1200 A.D. Each sample weighed about 100 mg.

The results from the labs were quite revealing. The Zurich lab was off 1,000 years because the samples were improperly cleaned of contamination. The other labs dated the Peruvian sample later than it actually was, between 1400 and 1668 A.D.

Similarly, in 1984, the body of an Iron Age man dubbed Lindow Man was found in the peat of Lindow Moss in Cheshire, England. The lab at Harwell, using the gas-counting radiocarbon-dating, initially dated the Lindow Man at 300 B.C. When small samples of skin were tested by Harwell and Oxford (which used the AMS technique), the former obtained a date of 500 A.D. and the latter 100 A.D. The age of the Lindow Man remains a mystery.

Likewise, in September 1991 the body of a young man was found in the glacier on the Austro-Italian border. Archaeologists determined he must have lived during the Bronze Age, circa 2000 B.C., because of the flanged metal ax and bow found near him. Laboratories in Oxford and Switzerland, using accelerated mass spectrometry, dated him at 3300 B.C. Another lab in Innsbruck tested grass associated with the man and concluded that he lived about 3000 B.C.

When Professor Wölfli tested a piece of a fifty-year-old linen tablecloth that belonged to his mother-in-law, the carbon-dating calculated it to be 350 years old![53]

Speaking at the Hong Kong symposium on the Shroud, Meacham listed a number of examples of erroneous dates given by Carbon-14 dating:

- Fish bone samples from Hong Kong known to be of Neolithic origin (at least 3000 years old) were dated to be less than 280 years old from the collagen fraction and 2110 years old from the carbonate fraction, while the Neolithic human remains from the same site had dates of less than 165 years for the carbonate and 800 years for the collagen.[54]
- Samples of wood from historical sites in the former Yugoslavia known to date back to the thirteenth century have given dates ranging from 240 and 580 years, while samples from the first and second century B.C. were dated as 2170, 6030 and 5600 years old.[55]
- The site of Akrotiri in Greece, destroyed by the Thera eruption around 1550 B.C. and covered with three meters of ash, was considered an ideal site for samples for radiocarbon dating. A series of eight samples provided only four results that were deemed "exceptionally early" and were out of the purview of the archaeological framework, while the other two dates were too recent and most likely contaminated.[56]
- A famous early site for man in North America is the Old Crow site in the Yukon territory of Canada. Radiocarbon tests done on bone tools from the site yielded disparate dates. Outer portions of the caribou rib tools dated around 27,000 years old while the inner portion of the bones produced a date of 1,350 years.[57]

## Summary

In summation, this chapter has examined a number of variables, human and natural, which can affect the results of Carbon-14 dating, indicating the method is not infallible and ought not be the sole litmus test used. Meacham put it well when he said:

> The fact that significant discrepancies do often result from contamination in [the] best sample materials from optimum archaeological conditions has major implications for C-14 measurement of the Shroud. First and foremost is the abandonment of any notion that a radiocarbon age of whatever magnitude will settle for all time the question of authenticity. Second, the choice of sampling sites on the relic should be governed by considerations of possible contamination and by the desirability of measuring both typical and atypical samples. Third, an elaborate pretreatment and screening program should be conducted before the samples are measured. Finally, the result should be interpreted to the general public in the light of contamination and other uncertainties inherent in the radiocarbon dating method.[58]

Clearly, a number of the factors elucidated by Meacham and others were not taken into consideration by the scientists in 1988 when they rendered their negative pronouncement on the Shroud.

# –10–
# Post-1988 Research

FOLLOWING the results of the 1988 C-14 test, the majority of people who read the negative headlines accepted the scientific proclamation without question. Those who were convinced that the Shroud was a fake now had their "proof." Many who were initially favorably disposed toward the authenticity of the Shroud were "converted" by science. As a consequence, interest in the Shroud began to wane almost immediately. However, not everyone was convinced by the C-14 test.

The Vatican made no comment concerning the results of the C-14 data other than they be published. It was not until August 18, 1990, after Cardinal Ballestrero* had retired and been succeeded by the new Archbishop of Turin, Cardinal Giovanni Saldarini, that a statement was made. Joaquin Navarro-Valles, the spokesman for the Holy See, remarked: "The medieval dating . . . is one that is in contrast to previous results. . . . This is one experimental datum among others with the validity and also the limits of such examinations, which ought to be integrated into a multidisciplinary framework."[1] This carefully phrased statement does not endorse ipso facto the results of the C-14 test, nor does it dismiss them outright; rather, it asserts that these results must be viewed within the context of other research. At that time the Vatican also invited proposals for further research. Cardinal

*Cardinal Ballestrero died on June 21, 1998.

Saldarini also announced that the Shroud would undergo new tests after the public exhibition in the year 2000.[2]

## Umbella of Pope John VII

A Congress on the Shroud was held in Bologna on May 6-7, 1989. It was officially opened by Cardinal Biffi, Archbishop of Bologna. The theme of the Congress was "The Holy Shroud and Icons." One of the presenters was the controversial Brother Bruno Bonnet-Eymard from France.[3] He delivered a paper in which he provided new evidence of the Shroud's existence at the beginning of the eighth century.

Pope John VII, who was Greek, reigned from 705-708. During his short pontificate, he had a chapel built with many Byzantine mosaics. One of the famous artifacts kept in the chapel was a relic known as the "Veil of Veronica." On solemn days when it was exposed for veneration, a richly embroidered umbella or canopy was used to adorn it. Although the umbella is no longer extant, a description and several sketches of the canopy by Jacopo Grimaldi can be found in a 1618 manuscript kept in the Vatican archives. Grimaldi's sketch depicts a dead Christ in the center of the embroidery and flanked by four Gospel scenes on either side. On one side, the Annunciation, various events associated with the Nativity, the Presentation of Our Lord and His Baptism are depicted. On the other side, the Transfiguration, Palm Sunday, the Crucifixion and the finding of the empty tomb by the women are depicted. Around the entire border are images of ecclesial and biblical personages. Three angels surround the perimeter of Our Lord's body.

Grimaldi's detailed sketch reveals that the original artist who designed Pope John VII's umbella had access to the Shroud.* Of particular note is the position of the hands over the private anatomy. Although Grimaldi adds a loincloth, this may have been done for reasons of modesty rather than as an accurate reproduction of the Shroud. This is a plausible supposition given that Grimaldi describes the embroidery as depicting Jesus *nudato corpore*, i.e., with "naked body." Also noteworthy is the fact that the right hand is placed over the left, which is like the Shroud when viewed with unaided eye. Furthermore, as on the Shroud, the thumb is not evident on the right hand.

## The Russian Scientists

Dr. Dmitri Kouznetsov, recipient of the Lenin Prize for Science, is a biochemist and former director of the E.A. Sedov Biopolymer Research Laboratories in Moscow who specializes in the archaeological dating of textiles. In 1991, while presenting a paper in London for the Egyptian Archaeological Society, he was approached by scientists from France and Belgium who requested that he apply his laboratory technique to determining the possibility of chemical contamination of the Shroud due to the fire of 1532. Kouznetsov, who acknowledges, "I am not a Shroud expert at all. . . . And before 1991, I didn't know anything about the Shroud itself,"[4] decided to accept their challenge.

Dr. Kouznetzov and his colleagues replicated the conditions of the 1532 fire in their lab using a piece of linen from En-Gedi, Israel, dated between B.C. 100–A.D. 100. Their study found that heat, melted silver, water and linen cellulose in the box can affect the cellulose

---

*Wilson associates the umbella with Pope Celestine III (1191-1198).

of the linen. The fire of 1532 lasted about six hours, and the temperature in the box was raised to approximately 960° C. After this experiment, the cloth was subjected to another C-14 test, and the resulting date was 1,200 years later, making the cloth much younger.

Kouznetsov does not dispute the results of the three labs who worked on the Shroud. He points out, "I completely agree with the measurements of radiocarbon dating made by colleagues from the three laboratories in 1989. . . . But I have some problems with their calculations."[5] He notes that the scientists did not take into account three factors:[6]

1. When flax is spun, the part made up of lipids and proteins, which contains less Carbon-14, is eliminated. Therefore, when linen is dated, it produces a much younger age than the flax plant itself.
2. The extreme temperature of the 1532 Chambery fire as well as carbon containing $CO^2$ and CO gases in the presence of water and silver induced a chemical process which led to an enrichment of C-14.
3. Microbes on the surface of the cloth cause a direct, chemical bonding of C-14 into the textile cellulose, which causes a chemical modification that cannot be removed by cleaning.

In another experiment, Kouznetsov and his colleagues tested a linen cloth from a dress belonging to a princess in Uzbekistan from between 760 A.D. and 840 A.D.[7] Using the same radiocarbon dating method as that used to date the Shroud, his laboratory came up with a date that ranged between 960 A.D. and 1070 A.D. When the cloth was put through conditions replicating the 1532 fire, it resulted in a date that was between 1210 A.D. and 1290 A.D., thus making it 400 years younger. Kouznetsov then applied an equation to correct for differences naturally found in flax and the effects of heat, and he came up with a date of 700 A.D. to 800 A.D.

When the Russian scientist applied this mathematical equation to the Shroud, he noted: "As a result of our current experimental study, we [believe] that the actual calendar age of the Shroud of Turin could be closer to the first or second century A.D. . . . Its *minimal* age, according to our calculations, is 1800 years."[8] Kouznetsov's data were quickly challenged by Jull, Donahue and Damon, who had carbon dated the Shroud back in 1988 at the Arizona lab.[9] They concluded that there were no observable changes in the C-14 age of the En-Gedi textile after it had been put through the replication of the fire of 1532, nor significant isotopic exchange of the textile under heat conditions. Jackson and Propp, in turn, rebutted the objections raised by Jull and his colleagues by citing that the conclusions reached by Kouznetsov were consistent with the attachment/exchange model they (Jackson and Propp) had developed.[10]

## Cloth-Collapse Theory

Dr. Jackson who has spent years attempting to explain how the image on the Shroud was formed, says: "Perhaps the reason why a satisfactory hypothesis has not been found is not so much due to a lack of image characterization but to an *overcharacterization*. That is, we seem to have a situation where the set of observables is so restrictive that all hypothesis posed thus far must be excluded.[11] He proposes a theory which contains certain aspects which do not fall within the range of conventional science but which is nonetheless scientifically well-posed and internally consistent. It is his conjecture that the cloth collapsed into and through the body, thus leaving the image on the Shroud.

Jackson posits that the body became mechanically "transparent" to its physical surroundings and that a stimulus such as radiation caused the image to be imprinted onto the cloth as it passed through the body. The points of the cloth that are closest to the body would have received the longest dose of radiation, while the points of the cloth which are further from the body would have received the least amount. As the cloth fell naturally by gravity, internal stresses within the cloth would have caused it to displace from the sides of the body and top of the head. Given that radiation is readily absorbed in air, no body images would have been imprinted in those areas.

According to Jackson, this theory adheres to standard principles of physics, namely, the cloth collapses under gravity, air absorbs radiation and cellulose is chemically modified by radiation. The only thing which contradicts accepted norms of physics is the action of the body itself.

## Fungi on the Shroud

Dr. Leoncio Garza-Valdes, a pediatrician and a microbiologist, visited Turin in May 1993, where he was introduced to Gonella and Riggi. While there, he was allowed to cut a thread from one of the samples of the Shroud which Riggi had taken back in 1988. This was apparently done without Cardinal Saldarini's permission. Upon examining the samples, Garza-Valdes found what he termed a "bioplastic coating," which is a microscopic layer of fungi and bacteria covering the threads. He took a small sample back with him to San Antonio. Engaging the assistance of colleagues in several universities, they were able to isolate three types of bacteria and four types of fungi. Of particular note was a pink-pigment-producing bacterium.[12] This is interesting because in 1978, members of the STURP team found pink material on their sticky tape samples which was believed to have been nylon, but in actuality it could have been this bacterium.

In September 1994, Dr. Garza-Valdes became an adjunct professor of microbiology at the University of Texas Health Science Center in San Antonio. Here he continued his research on the Shroud samples with the assistance of Professor Stephen Mattingly, a microbiologist, and Dr. Victor Tryon, director of the Center of Advanced DNA Technologies at the University.

Following the same cleaning procedure used by the three laboratories in 1988, namely, an "acid-base-acid" washing, Dr. Garza-Valdes noticed that "Nothing had changed. The fibers stayed the same; the bioplastic coating was still visible. . . . They intended to remove calcium carbonates, wax, and some of the organic material that was present. But the bacteria were not cleaned off. The bacteria on the Shroud grow in alkaline environments and were very happy that they were still being fed the sodium hydroxide solution."[13]

In a press release on May 5, 1995, Dr. Garza-Valdes stated:

> Microorganisms are known to form biogenic varnishes or protective coatings on desert rocks and other stable surfaces. Therefore, a study was undertaken to examine for similar microbial deposits, various ancient pre-Columbian artifacts . . . and also the Shroud of Turin. . . . In general, pigmented gram-positive cocci and pleomorphic rods and Lichenothelia fungi were found by microscopic and cultural analyses in all samples examined. In addition, a bioplastic material was produced by the bacteria that coated the surfaces. Cellulose digestion of a Shroud fragment resulted in the apparent diges-

> tion of the linen cellulose and release of glucose (determined by glucose oxidase). However, the microbial deposits (bioplastic-like coatings) on the linen, which were resistant to the enzyme, maintained the overall shape of the thread and appeared following digestion to have a hollow interior indicating the non-cellulose nature of the material covering the thread.
>
> An additional interesting finding on the Shroud of Turin is the presence of extreme haloalkaliphilic (having an affinity to high salt and high pH) bacteria tentatively classified as Natroanococcus, Natronobacterium, Nocardiopsis, and Synechocystis. These bacteria are significant because during the first century in the area of Palestine, natron (sodium carbonate) was used in the bleaching of linen and as an important ingredient in perfume and resins (myrrh).[14]

The presence of these bacteria, of which only about 10% is removed by the cleaning methods employed in 1988, could have produced further inaccuracies in the C-14 dating, thus making the Shroud appear younger than its actual age. Dr. Garza-Valdes asserts: "The Shroud of Turin result was abnormal because of the bioplastic coating. . . . I am convinced that at the present time, the radiocarbon dating of ancient textiles is not a reliable test."[15]

Interestingly, Dr. Gove, whose accelerator mass spectrometry (AMS) technology was used to carbon date the Shroud in 1988 and who accepted the 14th century date of the cloth, is now working with Dr. Garza-Valdes to perfect a method of carbon dating the actual cellulose of the Shroud linen without the bioplastic coating.

## DNA Testing

In October 1994, Dr. Victor Tryon and his wife Nancy conducted DNA testing on sample threads from the Shroud given him by Dr. Garza-Valdes. Using a technique called PCR (polymerase chain reaction), which multiplies the number of cells in a substance, they were able to identify three gene segments in the blood. Tryon found that the two samples contained human blood and male DNA, which was very degraded. According to Dr. Adler: "It's not surprising to find DNA. . . . It's hard to establish, however, that the DNA came from the specific blood sample you're working with. . . . With really old blood, the DNA does break down. You would get smears, instead of sharp bands."[16] Dr. Garza-Valdes admits that 95% of the blood areas on the Shroud are covered by fungi and bacteria, and the small amount of blood left will continue to disappear with the passage of time.[17] With numerous people handling the Shroud throughout the centuries it is virtually impossible to determine with absolute certitude if the DNA belongs to the same man whose image is on the cloth.

When this test result was made public, it immediately provoked controversy, for it was an unauthorized test. Even though the scientific test may have been carried out in an unbiased fashion, the Church does not accept the validity of these findings because the Pontifical Custodian of the Shroud was not apprised of these "secret" samples, nor was permission granted to conduct such a test. Cardinal Saldarini emphatically stated that "no new removal [of material from the Shroud] happened after April 21, 1988, and there should not be any residual material in the hands of a third party."[18] The Cardinal demanded that any circulating samples of the Shroud be returned to his custody.

## Flowers on the Shroud?

Oswald Scheuermann, a physics teacher in Germany who had conducted experiments in producing coronal type images with photography as well as on linen, noticed flower-like images around the face of the Shroud in his studies in 1983. Coronal type images are formed by a coronal discharge in which ionizing electrical energy spreads over the surface of an object in the electrical field. Afterward, sparks or ions tend to be discharged as streamers. The coronal type images are likely to come from pointed and irregular surfaces and margins. This was first noticed by Dr. Adler in 1982, when studying the coin-like objects over the eyes of the man on the Shroud.

> Where the object is in touch with the surfaces (Shroud, linen, photographic plate), the image tends to be dense. Where the object is partially in contact with the surface, the outline is dense and partial with a light central area. Objects which are further away from the surface or which are moist (with blood or sweat) tend to produce "shadow images" or "non-images."[19]

In 1985, Dr. Whanger examined a photograph of the Shroud with a magnifying glass and noticed what seemed like a large chrysanthemum flower on the anatomical left side of the cloth about 15 centimeters lateral to and 6 centimeters above the midline top of the head. He and his wife Mary obtained Michael Zohary's six volume set of *Flora Palestina*, which contains drawings of 1,900 plants. According to the Whangers, they identified 28 species of plants on the Shroud: 23 are flowers, three are small bushes, and two are thorns. The pollens of 25 of these flowers were previously noted by Dr. Frei in the 1970s. In addition to flowers, the Whangers state they have also noticed images of buds, stems, leaves and fruits on the Shroud: "The number of species of plants that we have identified ranged from 400 for Artimisia to only one species in the genus for three plants, the Gundelia, the Pteranthuxs and the Ridolphia."[20]

There are some skeptics who say that one can "see" whatever one is looking for on the Shroud, much like on a Rorschach inkblot. Among those who doubt that traces of flowers are visible on the Shroud is Rebecca Jackson. She states: "Jewish burial is supposed to be simple. No 'Mooktza' (untouchable items)—flowers, spears or sponges—were allowed to be buried with the body, as some have claimed."[21] The Whangers, however, point out examples of early portraits of Christ which depict flowers around His head. One such image comes from the third century and can be found in the Roman catacombs. Another is the sixth-century Pantocrator icon of St. Catherine's Monastery at Mt. Sinai, which has dozens of flower images in the halo around the head. Even more telling are the replicas of flowers on the gold solidus coins struck between 692-695 A.D. by order of Justinian II. Similarly, the gold coins issued by Constantine VII in 950 A.D. also bear images of flowers modeled after the Mandylion.

In 1995 the Whangers sought the assistance of Avinoam Danin, a botany professor from Hebrew University in Jerusalem. He was able to demonstrate that 96% of the flower species identified on the Shroud grow around Jerusalem and the Qumran Caves region. If one were to include the southern Dead Sea area in the calculation, then 100% of the specimens can be found. Serendipitously, these flowers only bloom during the Easter season. Danin and his colleague, Dr. Uri Baruch, a palynologist with the Israel Antiquities Authority, found that the most frequent pollen type (29.1%) is that of *Gundelia tournefortii,* a spiny plant believed by some to have been used for the crown of thorns.[22] Interestingly, two pollen grains of this species were also discovered on the sticky tape samples from the Sudarium of Oviedo. According to Danin: "The assemblage of plants . . . shows [the Shroud] could only come from the Middle East, and the best fit is Jerusalem."[23]

## Codex Vossianus Latinus Q 69

Gino Zaninotto, the historian and expert in archaeology who discovered a copy of the Greek manuscript which contained the sermon given by Gregory the archdeacon on the occasion of the arrival of the Shroud at Constantinople in 944 A.D., made another significant discovery. In a paper presented at the International Symposium on the Shroud in June 1993, Zaninotto reported that he had found a tenth-century manuscript known as the *Codex Vossianus Latinus Q 69.*[24] This document makes reference to an eighth-century account of Syrian origin which relates that Jesus left the imprint of His entire body on a cloth kept in the great church in Edessa. This is a clear reference to the Shroud.

## The Corporal/Antimension and the Shroud

An interesting study was made by Fr. Hilary Conti, O.S.B., on the origin of the use of the corporal and the antimension for the celebration of the Eucharist.[25] A corporal is a white, square, linen cloth upon which the Body and Blood of the Lord are placed during the Eucharistic Liturgy. Of the eighteen rites within the Catholic Church, Fr. Conti found that all make use of a corporal or antimension or something equivalent.

The earliest mention of a corporal and its connection to the Shroud can be found in the *Liber Pontificalis* in which Pope Sylvester I decreed in 325 A.D. that "the Sacrifice of the Mass should be offered on linen . . . as the Body of Christ was buried in a clean linen shroud." In the Eastern tradition, it is piously believed that seven days after the Resurrection of Our Lord, St. James celebrated the Eucharist on the actual burial cloth of Christ.

Fr. Conti notes it is quite probable that only one linen cloth, serving as both altar cloth and corporal, was used in the early centuries of the Church. The corporal was referred to by various names: *palla corporalis* ("mantle of the body"), *velamen dominicae mensae* ("veil of the table of the Lord"), or *opertorium dominici corporis* ("cover of the body of the Lord"). In the fourteenth century, the size of the linen was shortened to make two pieces; one half was called the "corporal," which was used on the altar, and the other half became the *palla* or "pall," which is used to cover the chalice.

The antimension is the Eastern Church's version of the Latin corporal; sacred relics are sewn into the antimension. While the corporal always remained a clean linen cloth, by the late Middle Ages the antimension was decorated with the image of the dead Body of Christ. Similarly, in the Orthodox Church, the antimension is replaced on Great Friday or Good Friday with a cloth known simply as "the Shroud," because it has an image much like that seen on the Shroud of Turin.

Given the long tradition of the use of a corporal or antimension within each rite of the Church, one can reasonably conclude that this cloth is of apostolic origin, with connections to the Shroud of Christ.

## Fire of April 11–12, 1997

For the second time in 465 years, the Shroud was heroically saved from destruction. On the night of April 11, 1997, while a gala dinner was being held in the Royal Palace adjacent to the Cathedral of San Giovanni where the Shroud is housed in its Guarini Chapel, fire alarms went off shortly after 11 p.m. The custodians went to check the Cathedral but found no evidence of smoke or fire. It was not until 11:35 p.m. that the parish priest, Fr. Francesco Barbero, called the fire department. According to another account, the first phone call to the fire department was made by a Turin citizen, Guido Principe. Approximately 200 firemen came to the scene and battled the blaze until 4:30 a.m.

The Guarini Chapel, which was festooned with scaffolding for renovation work, was heavily damaged. The Shroud, which was kept in a silver reliquary behind two-inch-thick layers of bulletproof glass, was retrieved by a fireman named Mario Trematore. It was carried out of the Cathedral at 1:36 a.m., two hours after the first phone call to the fire department. Unlike the fire of 1532 in Chambery, France, in which the cloth was scorched, this time it remained unscathed. Authorities have ruled out the possibility of the fire being started by an electrical short circuit. The more probable cause seems to be arson.

Eleven days after the blaze, an awards ceremony was held for the valiant efforts of the law enforcement and fire departments. During the presentation, Cardinal Saldarini expressed his personal opinion concerning the Shroud: "I am convinced that the Shroud wrapped the body of Jesus."[26]

## 1998 Exhibition

The Shroud was on display for the third time in the twentieth century from April 18 to June 14, 1998. The year marked several important events in Turin's history: it was the 1600th anniversary of the first Council of Turin, the 500th anniversary of the dedication of the new Cathedral, and the 100th anniversary of the first photograph of the Shroud by Secondo Pia.

In the early morning hours of April 15, the Shroud was accompanied by the Archbishop of Turin, Cardinal Saldarini, and taken from an undisclosed place to the sacristy of the Cathedral. Also present were Mechtilde Flury-Lemberg, the textile expert, and Sister Maria Clara, who removed the old blue satin border and stitched the Shroud onto a white cloth as a support for its display. On April 17, the Shroud was placed in a new case weighing three tons and made of bulletproof glass. The case was equipped with a combination of inert gas and steam and was kept at a temperature about 18° C. The first guests to view the Shroud on April 18, the opening day of the exhibition, were Cardinal Saldarini, Princess Maria Gabriella of Savoy and her daughter Elisabetta. Later that morning a press conference was held with over 800 journalists from around the world. A solemn Mass with many Piedmontese bishops was celebrated at 4:00 p.m.

The Third International Congress for Shroud Studies, which this author attended, was held during this exhibition period from June 5-7. The theme for this congress was "The Shroud and Science." The Congress was officially opened on June 5 by Cardinal Saldarini in the presence of the President of the Republic of Italy, Oscar Luigi Scalfaro.

Those who had been looking forward to this Congress in hopes of learning new information on the Shroud were sorely disappointed. It appeared that anyone who submitted a title for presentation was accepted. Thus there were 104 papers presented in two and one half days. Given the time restriction, each individual was initially allotted eight minutes to speak, which soon became four minutes when it became apparent that even eight minutes was too much time to allow for each researcher. Consequently, presenters who had spent years in research were disappointed in not being able to present their data adequately, and attendees who were expecting to hear substantive reporting were discontented.

## Jubilee Year 2000

The Shroud was exposed at the Cathedral of Turin for a ten-week period (the longest in history) from August 12–October 22, 2000 in commemoration of the Redemption. Archbishop Severino Poletto officially opened the public exposition.*

In a message sent by Pope John Paul II on August 13, the Holy Father said: "It is difficult to remain indifferent before the Holy Shroud. Indeed, the face speaks to the intelligence and heart. It speaks to the believer, the seeker, and the nonbeliever."

---

*In June 1999 Cardinal Saldarini resigned as Archbishop of Turin due to health problems. Pope John Paul II appointed Bishop Severino Poletto, Bishop of Asti, as the new Archbishop and made him a Cardinal on February 21, 2001.

# Afterword

IN this book I have attempted to investigate the Shroud from the viewpoints of various disciplines: historical, biblical, ecclesiastical and scientific. From the historical vantage point, it has been duly noted that an image of what is now called the Shroud of Turin was probably known in the ancient world as the Mandylion or the Holy Napkin. While some part of its history may be shrouded in legend, one cannot dismiss outright the fact that an oral story regarding a mysterious image of a bearded man was circulating from around 31 A.D.

Studying the Shroud from a biblical perspective, we have examined the Gospels and found that much of what the Evangelists say about the manner and death of Jesus of Nazareth is visibly reflected on this cloth. The similarities between the scriptural accounts and the sufferings depicted on the man of the Shroud are too numerous to be discounted as pure coincidence.

With regard to the ecclesiastical position on the Shroud, the Church has always permitted its veneration by the faithful as a pious devotion. Popes throughout history have encouraged devotion to this sacred image and granted indulgences to those who would pray before it. As early as the 8th century, Pope Stephen III spoke of the Shroud in one of his homilies shortly after being elected Supreme Pontiff.

Scientific studies have been made of the Shroud following the first photographs taken in 1898 by Secondo

Pia. The first person to conduct a serious scientific analysis of the Shroud was the Frenchman, Paul Vignon, in 1900. Based upon his experiments he concluded that the image on the cloth was not a painting. In the 1930s, Dr. Pierre Barbet made a comprehensive anatomical study of the Shroud and was awestruck at how accurately the wounds, blood and other bodily fluids represented on the man of the Shroud reflect one who has indeed suffered tremendous torture and the horrendous death of crucifixion. Further studies by pathologists later in the century have affirmed that the wound marks are accurate to the minutest detail—information which would not have been known by a forger or one who practiced medicine in the Middle Ages.

In 1978, the Shroud of Turin Research Project (STURP), composed of over 30 scientists of various disciplines and religious traditions, conducted countless tests on the Shroud for 120 hours. Among their findings, they concluded that the image of the man on the Shroud was not painted and that the image was only on the uppermost fibers of the cloth. If the image were a painting, the paint would penetrate the cloth; this is clearly not the case with the Shroud. Perhaps the most interesting find is the three-dimensional quality of the image of the man on the Shroud. A typical painting is two-dimensional. This means that the cloth actually covered a human body.

The most widely known scientific test on the Shroud, which has spurred controversy at all levels, is the 1988 Carbon-14 test, the result of which claimed the date of the Shroud to be between 1260-1390. As was examined in this book, the 1988 Carbon-14 testing was fraught with irregularities which warrant a dismissal of those results. These irregularities include the breach of protocol and the lack of a true blind test, the selection of a contaminated sample site, the handling of the cloth without sterile gloves, and the use of only three laboratories—who employed the same technique—plus evidence of partiality. Most importantly, we must take into account the unreliability of radiocarbon dating itself.

While many have accepted the radiocarbon date without question, we have shown that radiocarbon dating is a fallible tool for testing. Radiocarbon dates have been known to be off at least 1,000 years! With radiocarbon testing, two factors are presumed: first, the uniform distribution of Carbon-14 in the atmosphere, and secondly, the atmospheric origin of the carbon found in living organisms. These cannot be guaranteed with respect to the Shroud of Turin. Notwithstanding these presumptions, there are also many extraneous variables which could have skewed the radiocarbon test. Throughout its long history the Shroud has been mishandled, subjected to smoke from incense, fire and candles, as well as to humidity, bacteria, wax and other unknown contaminants. To obtain an accurate radiocarbon date, these residues would have to be completely cleaned from a sample before testing. It is known that the chemicals used in the 1988 Carbon-14 test of the Shroud did not clean the samples thoroughly. As a result, the samples were tested with contaminants and thus produced an inaccurate date of origin for the Shroud. With new advancements in scientific technology it is hoped that the Shroud of Turin can be tested again at some future time and a more accurate date be given for its origin.

What is more, Carbon-14 testing must take its place among the other forms of scientific testing, and these clearly point toward the Shroud's authenticity. In addition to the extensive anatomical and chemical studies of the marks on the Shroud, as well as a multitude of technical analyses of the image itself, further tests have yielded evidence of Palestinian pollen grains, of pre-medieval inscriptions and of the impress of coins from the reign of Pontius Pilate. Added to this is the historical evidence, including the similarity of the image to early Byzantine portraits of the Holy Face and the discovery of medieval artifacts recording the existence of the Shroud. All these compelling data have been accumulated over a long period of time by a cross section of researchers, professional and amateur, of disparate backgrounds.

When dealing with the Shroud of Turin it is difficult to come to a truly definitive conclusion, for we are dealing in the realm of mystery. In this book I have examined some of the major research findings supporting the case for the authenticity of the Shroud of Turin as the burial cloth of Jesus Christ. The Church can never oblige the faithful to accept this position, for the Shroud is not part of the Deposit of Faith. As Pope John Paul II stated in Turin on the occasion of his visit on May 24, 1998: "Since it is not a matter of faith, the Church has no specific competence to pronounce on these questions. She entrusts to scientists the task of continuing to investigate, so that satisfactory answers may be found to the questions connected with this Sheet." (*L'Osservatore Romano*, May 27, 1998).

Science, at its best, has limitations. However, science can aid in one's understanding of the Faith by shedding light on the facts of history. The insights of science on the Shroud of Turin can contribute in leading man toward God and toward the Saviour, Jesus Christ. For the time being, may the mystery of the Shroud inspire those who gaze upon its image to seek the face of God.

# Notes

## Chapter 1
## HISTORY OF THE SHROUD

1. Eusebius Pamphili, *Ecclesiastical History*, Book I, Ch. 13, trans. Roy J. Deferrari (New York: The Fathers of the Church, Inc., 1953), p. 77.
2. *Ibid.*, p. 80.
3. Ian Wilson, *The Shroud of Turin* (New York: Image Books, 1979), p. 120, and endnote 16 on p. 307.
4. Kenneth E. Stevenson and Gary R. Habermas, *Verdict on the Shroud* (Ann Arbor, MI: Servant Books, 1981), p. 24.
5. Procopius of Caesarea, *Buildings* II, Ch. 7, trans. H. B. Dewing (Cambridge, MA: Harvard University Press, 1961), p. 143.
6. Wilson, pp. 139, 144.
7. *Ibid.*, p. 140.
8. Theodoret and Evagrius, *History of the Church* (London: Henry G. Bohn, 1884), p. 407.
9. Cf. note 4 in Wilson, Ch. 12.
10. A. M. Dubarle, O.P., *Storia Antica della Sindone di Torino fino al XIII secolo* (Roma: Edizioni Giovinezza, 1986), p. 88.
11. Bishop John Kallos, *What About the Holy Mandylion and Turin Shroud?* (MN: Light and Life Publishing Company, 1991), p. 4.
12. Daniel C. Scavone, "The History of the Turin Shroud to the 14th Century," *Symposium Proceedings: History, Science, Theology and the Shroud*, St. Louis, MO, June 22-23, 1991 (Amarillo, TX: The Man in the Shroud Committee of Amarillo, 1991), p. 192.
13. Gino Zaninotto, "Orazione di Gregorio il Referendario in Occasione della Traslazione a Constantinopli dell'Imagine Edessena nell'anno 944," in *La Sindone: Indagini Scientifiche* (Milano: Edizioni Paoline, 1988), p. 344.
14. Orazio Petrosillo and Emanuela Marinelli, *The Enigma of the Shroud* (Malta: Publishers Enterprise Group, 1996), p. 177.
15. Scavone, p. 192.
16. Stevenson and Habermas, p. 24.
17. Wilson, p. 167.

18. *Ibid.*, pp. 167-168.
19. *Ibid.*, p. 169.
20. *Ibid.*, p. 173.
21. *Ibid.*, p. 175.
22. Rex Morgan, "Did the Templars Take the Shroud to England? New Evidence from Templecombe," *History, Science, Theology and the Shroud*, p. 211.
23. *Ibid.*, p. 215.
24. Brother Bruno Bonnet-Eymard of the Little Brothers of the Sacred Heart, "Study of Original Documents of the Archives of the Diocese of Troyes in France with particular Reference to the Memorandum of Pierre d'Arcis," *History, Science, Theology and the Shroud*, p. 242.
25. Rev. Patrick O'Connell, B.D. and Rev. Charles Carty, *The Holy Shroud and Four Visions* (Rockford, IL: TAN Books and Publishers, Inc., rpt. 1974), pp. 8-9.
26. Wilson, p. 212.
27. Bonnet-Eymard, p. 244.
28. *Ibid.*, pp. 266-267.
29. *Ibid.*, p. 207.
30. Ulysse Chevalier, *Etude critique sur l'origine du Saint Suaire de Lirey-Chambery-Turin* (Paris: Picard, 1900), Appendix H, p. XII.
31. Luigi Fossati, "The Lirey Controversy," *Shroud Spectrum International*, No. 8, September 1983, p. 28.
32. Bonnet-Eymard, pp. 237-238.
33. Fossati, p. 28.
34. Luigi Fossati, "From Object of Devotion to Object of Discussion," *Shroud Spectrum International*, No. 37, December 1990, p. 9.
35. Wilson, p. 212.
36. Andre Chagny, "An Exposition of the Holy Shroud in the Market Place of Bourg-en-Bresse, 14 April 1503," *Shroud Spectrum International*, No. 37, December 1990, p. 5.
37. *Ibid.*
38. Brother Bruno Bonnet-Eymard, "The Holy Shroud, Silent Witness," *The Catholic Counter-Reformation in the XXth Century* (hereafter, *CRC*), No. 295, April 1997, p. 18.
39. G. B. Rossi, *La SS. Sindon* (Torino-Roma: Marietti, 1931), for data up to 1931.
40. Secondo Pia, "The First Photograph of the Holy Shroud," *Sindon*, April 1960.
41. Francis Conklin, "The Holy Shroud," *From the Housetops*, No. 37, 1995, p. 9.

## Chapter 2
## POPES AND THE SHROUD

1. Wilson, p. 158.
2. *Ibid.*, p. 109.
3. Caesar Gili, *In the Splendor of His Countenance* (Newark, NJ, 1990), p. 7.
4. *Ibid.*, p. 8.
5. Wilson, p. 217.
6. Gili, p. 9.
7. Wilson, p. 221.
8. Benedict XIV, *De servorum Dei beatificatione et de beatorum canonizatione* (Bologna, 1738), pp. 307 ff.
9. Gili, p. 10.
10. *Ibid.*, p. 7.
11. Mark Fellows, *A Second Coming: The Holy Shroud in the 20th Century* (St. Paul, MN: The Remnant Press, 1996), p. 7.
12. *Ibid.*, p. 11.
13. Pierre Barbet, M.D., *A Doctor at Calvary* (New York: Image Books, 1963), pp. 10-11.
14. Gili, p. 11.
15. *Ibid.*
16. *Insegnamenti di Paolo VI*: Vol. XI, 1973 (Vatican City: Tipografia Poliglotta Vaticana, 1973), pp. 1138-1139.
17. *Shroud Spectrum International*, March 1982, p. 34.
18. *Ibid.*
19. *L'Osservatore Romano* (Italian ed.), April 14-15, 1980, p. 4.
20. *L'Osservatore Romano* (Italian ed.), April 21-22, 1980, p. 2.
21. Greg Burke, "The Shroud of Turin," *Columbia* (New Haven, CT), June 1998, p. 4.
22. *L'Osservatore Romano*, "The Shroud Whispers: Believe in God's Love and Flee from the Misfortune of Sin," May 27, 1998, p. 4.

## Chapter 3
## SCRIPTURE AND THE SHROUD

1. Louis F. Hartman, C.SS.R., *Encyclopedic Dictionary of the Bible* (New York: McGraw-Hill Book Company, Inc., 1963), p. 287.
2. Raymond E. Brown, S.S., *The Gospel According to John*: XIII-XXI (New York: Doubleday, 1970), p. 942. [Publisher's Note: Fr. Brown is being cited here not on doctrinal matters but for his views on various points of ancient history and language.]
3. Thomas Humber, *The Sacred Shroud* (NY: Pocket Books, 1978), p. 68.

4. Raymond E. Brown, S.S., *The Death of the Messiah*, Vol. II (New York: Doubleday, 1994), p. 1243.
5. Rabbi Solomon Ganzfried, *Code of Jewish Law*, translated by Hyman E. Goldin, LL.B. (New York: Hebrew Publishing Company, 1961), pp. 99-100.
6. Wilson, p. 56.
7. Raymond E. Brown, S.S., *The Gospel of St. John: The Johannine Epistles* (Collegeville, MN: The Liturgical Press, 1960), pp. 92-93.
8. Brown, *The Death of the Messiah*, Vol. II, p. 1264.
9. Rabbi Dan Cohn-Sherbok, "The Jewish Shroud of Turin?" in *The Expository Times*, October 1980, Vol. 92, No. 1, p. 15.
10. Wilfrid Harrington, O.P., *Mark* (Wilmington, Delaware: Michael Glazier, 1988), p. 213.
11. Robert H. Gundry, *Mark: A Commentary on His Apology for the Cross* (Grand Rapids, Michigan: William B. Eerdmans Publishing Company, 1993), p. 814.
12. Raymond E. Brown, S.S., *The Gospel According to John: I-XII* (New York: Doubleday, 1966), p. 454.
13. Brown, *The Gospel of St. John: The Johannine Epistles*, p. 62.
14. Ganzfried, p. 99.
15. *Ibid.*, p. 50.
16. Werner Bulst, S.J., *The Shroud of Turin* (Milwaukee: The Bruce Publishing Company, 1957), p. 95.
17. Barbet, pp. 173-74.
18. Brown, *The Gospel According to John: XIII-XXI,* p. 942.
19. Brown, *The Death of the Messiah,* Vol. II, p. 1255.
20. Peter M. Rinaldi, *It Is the Lord* (New York: Warner Books, 1973), p. 28.
21. Edward A. Wuenschel, *Self-Portrait of Christ: The Holy Shroud of Turin* (Esopus, NY: Holy Shroud Guild, 1957), p. 49.
22. Barbet, p. 92.
23. Charlene Scott, "The Shroud of Turin: Who Is This Man?" in *Holy Shroud Research Continues in Colorado* (Colorado Springs, CO: Sindone Press, 1994), p. 16.
24. Barbet, pp. 97-98.
25. *Ibid.*, p. 131.
26. *Ibid.*, pp. 134, 135.
27. *Ibid.*, p. 136.
28. *Ibid.*, p. 139.

## Chapter 4
## THE SUDARIUM OF OVIEDO

1. Mark Guscin, *The Oviedo Cloth* (Great Britain: Redwood Books, 1998), p. 14.
2. *Ibid.*, p. 17.

3. San Braulio de Zaragoza, Letter 42, in *Patrologia Latina*, Vol. 80, Ed. J. P. Migne., trans. Fr. Thomas Buffer (Paris: *apud editorem*, 1850), col. 689.
4. Guscin, p. 22.
5. Alan D. Whanger and Mary W. Whanger, "A Comparison of the Sudarium of Oviedo and the Shroud of Turin Using the Polarized Image Overlay Technique," *Sudario del Señor: Actas del I Congresso Internacional sobre El Sudario de Oviedo* (Universidad de Oviedo, 1996), p. 380.
6. Carmen Gomez Ferreras, *"El Sudario de Oviedo y la Palinologia," Sudario del Señor,* p. 86.
7. *Ibid.*, pp. 88-89.
8. Guscin, p. 22.
9. *Ibid.*, p. 23.
10. Whanger, "A Quantitative Optical Technique for Analyzing and Authenticating the Images on the Shroud of Turin, p. 312.
11. *The Holy Shroud Guild Newsletter*, December 25, 1999, p. 3.
12. Jose Delfin Villalain Blanco, *"Estudio Hematologico Forense Realizado Sobre el 'Santo Sudario' de Oviedo," Sudario del Señor,* p. 149.
13. Guscin, p. 46.
14. *Ibid.*
15. *Ibid.*
16. Fr. Nicola Nasuti, O.F.M. Conv., *The Eucharistic Miracle of Lanciano* (Lanciano: Litografia Botolini srl, 1988), p. 73.
17. Giulio Ricci, *"L'Uomo della Sindone è Gesù"* (Roma: Studium, 1969).
18. Jorge-Manuel Rodriguez Almenar, *"Otros Datos Historicos Sobre el Sudario: Pasado, presente y futuro del Lienzo de Oviedo," Sudario del Señor,* p. 120.

## Chapter 5
## SCIENTIFIC STUDIES: 1898-1973

1. Paul Vignon, D.Sc., *The Shroud of Christ* (New York: University Books, 1970), p. 28.
2. *Ibid.*, p. 30.
3. *Ibid.*, p. 131ff.
4. *Ibid.*, pp. 165, 169.
5. Wilson, pp. 33-34.
6. Walter McCrone, *Judgement Day for the Turin Shroud* (Chicago, IL: Microscope Publications, 1997), p. 7.
7. *Ibid.*, p. 10.
8. *Ibid.*, p. 17.
9. *Ibid.*, p. 12.
10. *Ibid.*, pp. 18, 19.
11. Max Frei, "Nine Years of Palinological Studies on the Shroud," *Shroud Spectrum International,* No. 3, June 1982, p. 5.

## Chapter 6
## THE 1978 STURP STUDY

1. Pierluigi Baima Bollone, Maria Jorio & Anna Lucia Massaro, "Identification of the Group of the Traces of Human Blood on the Shroud," *Shroud Spectrum International*, No. 6, March 1983, p. 3.
2. John Heller and Alan Adler, "A Chemical Investigation of the Shroud of Turin," *Canadian Society for Forensic Science Journal*, Vol. 14, #3, 1981, p. 92.
3. Thomas W. Case, *The Shroud of Turin and the C-14 Fiasco* (Cincinnati: White Horse Press, 1996), p. 57.
4. Marc Borkan, "Ecce Homo? Science and the Authenticity of the Turin Shroud," *Vertices,* Winter 1995, Vol. X, No. 2, p. 22.
5. Heller and Adler, p. 96.
6. Dr. John H. Heller, *Report on the Shroud of Turin* (Boston: Houghton Mifflin Company, 1983), p. 152.
7. Joseph A. Kohlbeck and Eugenia L. Nitowski, "New Evidence May Explain Image on Shroud of Turin," *Biblical Archaeology Review*, July/August 1986, Vol. XII, No. 4, p. 23.
8. Frank C. Tribbe, *Portrait of Jesus?* (New York: Stein and Day/Publishers, 1983), p. 208.

## Chapter 7
## THE CASE AGAINST AUTHENTICITY

1. *The New York Times*, February 13, 1996, p. C-11.
2. *Ibid.*, p. C-1.
3. Walter McCrone, *Judgement Day for the Turin Shroud* (Chicago: Microscope Publications, 1997), p. 100.
4. Rodney Hoare, *The Turin Shroud Is Genuine* (New York: Barnes & Noble Books, 1995), p. 48.
5. McCrone, p. 103.
6. Stevenson and Habermas, *The Shroud and the Controversy*, p. 121.
7. Heller, p. 216.
8. R. A. Morris, L. A. Schwalbe, and J. R. London, "X-Ray Fluorescence Investigation of the Shroud of Turin," *X-ray Spectrometry*, Vol. 9, No. 2, 1980, p. 40.
9. L. A. Schwalbe and R. N. Rogers, "Physics and Chemistry of the Shroud of Turin," *Analytica Chimica Acta*, Vol. 135, 1982, p. 39.
10. Clive Prince, "Did Leonardo da Vinci Fake the Shroud?," Talk by Lynn Picknett, *British Society for the Turin Shroud Newsletter*, No. 28, April/May 1991, p. 12.
11. Isabel Piczek, "Why Leonardo da Vinci Could Not Have Painted The Shroud," *British Society for the Turin Shroud Newsletter*, No. 28, April/May 1991, p. 15.

12. Isabel Piczek, "Is the Turin Shroud a Painting?," *History, Science, Theology and the Shroud*, p. 262.
13. Gilbert R. Lavoie, *Unlocking the Secrets of the Shroud* (Allen, Texas: Thomas More, 1998), p. 62.
14. Heller, p. 194.
15. Piczek, p. 263.
16. *Ibid.*, p. 265.
17. *Ibid.*, 266.
18. Humber, p. 183.
19. *Ibid.*, pp. 183-184.
20. Stevenson and Habermas, 1981, p. 90.
21. Humber, p. 198.
22. Heller, p. 220.
23. Stevenson and Habermas, 1990, p. 131.
24. *Ibid.*, p. 40.
25. *Ibid.*, p. 177.
26. *Shroud Spectrum International*, No. 13, December 1984, p. 3.
27. Heller, p. 210.
28. Joe Nickell, *Inquest on the Shroud of Turin* (New York: Prometheus Books, 1983), p. 80.
29. Stevenson and Habermas, 1990, p. 31.
30. Isabel Piczek, "Art and the Shroud: Shroud Image Not So Easily Explained," *The Holy Shroud Guild Newsletter*, July 14, 1995, Vol. #2, No. 51, p. 4.
31. Heller, p. 209.
32. Stevenson and Habermas, 1990, pp. 31-32.
33. Heller, p. 203.

## Chapter 8
## THE CASE FOR AUTHENTICITY

1. *The Silent Witness* (Santa Monica, CA: Pyramid Film and Video, 1978).
2. Barbara Stinson Lee, "Shroud Research Reveals Intact Muscle Fragment," *Intermountain Catholic*, March 21, 1997, p. 5.
3. Frederick T. Zugibe, Ph.D., M.D., *The Cross and the Shroud* (New York: Exposition Press, 1982), pp. 195-196.
4. Barbet, p. 119.
5. Frederick T. Zugibe, M.D., Ph.D., "Pierre Barbet Revisited," *Sindon*, No. 8, December 1995, p. 110.
6. *Ibid.*, p. 113.
7. Lavoie, p. 188.
8. Msgr. G. Ricci, *The Way of the Cross . . . in the Light of The Holy Shroud* (Rome: Centro Romano di Sindonologia, 1978), p. 64.
9. Wilson, p. 42.
10. Zugibe, *The Cross and the Shroud*, p. 88.

11. Barbet, p. 128.
12. Nicu Haas, "Anthropological Observations on the Skeletal Remains from Giv'at ha'Mivtar," *Israel Exploration Journal*, Vol. 20, 1970, pp. 38-59.
13. CRC, No. 295, April 1997, p. 11.
14. A. Lebec, "A Physiological Study of the Passion of Our Lord Jesus Christ," *The Catholic Medical Guardian*, 1925.
15. Barbet, p. 85.
16. Zugibe, "Pierre Barbet Revisited," pp. 113-14.
17. *Ibid.*, p. 114.
18. Barbet, p. 109.
19. S. L. Robins, R. S. Cotran and V. Kumar, *Pathologic Basis of Disease*, 3rd Edition (Philadelphia: W. B. Saunders & Co., 1984), p. 138.
20. Barbet, p. 134.
21. *Ibid.*, p. 129.
22. Stevenson and Habermas, 1981, p. 136.
23. Humber, pp. 150-151.
24. Jerome S. Goldblatt, "The Shroud," *National Review*, April 16, 1982, p. 416.
25. Lavoie, p. 111.
26. N. Cinquemani, *A Medical Inquiry into the Crucifixion: The Double Images on the Shroud of Turin* (Roma: Edizioni Giovinezza, 1997), p. 10.
27. Werner Bulst, S.J., "The Pollen Grains on the Shroud of Turin," *Shroud Spectrum International*, No. 10, March 1984, p. 24.
28. Brother Bruno Bonnet-Eymard, "One Year After the Verdict of the 13 October 1988: The Victory of the Holy Shroud Won by Science," *CRC*, September-October 1989, No. 223, p. 20.
29. *CRC*, August-September 1986, No. 192, p. 21.
30. *Ibid.*
31. Frei, p. 7.
32. Mary and Alan Whanger, *The Shroud of Turin: An Adventure of Discovery* (TN: Providence House Publishers, 1998), p. 79.
33. *CRC*, No. 192, p. 21.
34. Ian Wilson, *The Blood and the Shroud* (New York: The Free Press, 1998), p. 104.
35. Wilson, 1978, p. 63.
36. *The Blood and the Shroud*, p. 103.
37. *Chicago Sun Times*, November 12, 1979, p. 12.
38. Dr. Alan D. Whanger, "A Reply to Doubts Concerning the Coins over the Eyes," *The Holy Shroud Guild Newsletter*, December 1997, Vol. #3, No. 56, p. 7.
39. Mario Moroni, "Pontius Pilate's Coin on the Right Eye of the Man in the Holy Shroud," *History, Science, Theology and the Shroud*, p. 283ff.

40. Alan Whanger and Mary Whanger, "Polarized Image Overlay Technique: A New Image Comparison Method and Its Application," *Applied Optics*, 24 (March 1985), p. 771.
41. *The Shroud of Turin: An Adventure of Discovery*, p. 28.
42. Alan D. Whanger, M.D. and Mrs. Mary W. Whanger, "A Quantitative Optical Technique for Analyzing and Authenticating the Images on the Shroud of Turin," *History, Science, Theology and the Shroud*, p. 321.
43. *Ibid.*, p. 322.
44. *Inside the Vatican*, October 1996, pp. 20-21.
45. *The Shroud of Turin: An Adventure of Discovery*, p. 28.
46. *Ibid.*, 24.
47. Werner Bulst, S.J., "Who Is the Man on the Shroud?" (Darmstadt, Germany, June 1984), reprinted in *The Holy Shroud Guild Newsletter*, May 21, 1996, Vol. #1, No. 53, p. 4.
48. Wilson, 1979, pp. 104-105.
49. "A Quantitative Optical Technique for Analyzing and Authenticating the Images on the Shroud of Turin," p. 308, and *The Shroud of Turin: An Adventure of Discovery*, p. 33.
50. "A Quantitative Optical Technique . . .," p. 307.
51. *Ibid.*, p. 306.
52. *Ibid.*, p. 307.
53. A. M. Dubarle, O.P., *Storia Antica della Sindone di Torino fino al XIII secolo* (Roma: Edizioni Giovinezza, 1986), pp. 48-51.
54. Jerome Lejeune, "Unfolding the Shroud," *The Catholic World Report*, July 1994, pp. 51-52.
55. *Ibid.*, p. 52.
56. Mario Cappi, *La Sindone dalla A alla Z: Storia, Scienza, Fede* (Padova: Messagero Di S. Antonio, 1997), p. 352.
57. *Ibid.*, p. 354.
58. *Ibid.*
59. *Ibid.*, p. 355.
60. Orazio Petrosillo e Emanuela Marinelli, *La Sindone: Storia di Un Enigma* (Milano: Rizzoli, 1998), p. 109.
61. *Ibid.*, p. 110.
62. *Ibid.*
63. Stefania Falasca with Stefano Gasseri, "Satanism: More and More Widespread Among Catholics," *30 Days*, No. 5, 1996, p. 38.
64. Rossana Ansuini, "Italy: And Turin Triples Its Exorcists," *30 Days*, No. 1, January 1989, p. 61.
65. *Ibid.*

## Chapter 9
## 1988 CARBON-14 CONTROVERSY

1. *L'Osservatore Romano* (English edition), 17 October 1988, p. 2.
2. Petrosillo and Marinelli, p. 22.
3. William Meacham, "Radiocarbon Measurement and the Age of the Turin Shroud: Possibilities and Uncertainties," from the proceedings of the symposium "Turin Shroud—Image of Christ?" (Hong Kong, 1986), p. 52.
4. Petrosillo and Marinelli, p. 28.
5. Giovanni Riggi diNumana, *Rapporto Sindone 1978-1987* (3M Edizioni, 1988), p. 150.
6. Ian Anderson, "Vatican Undermines Test on Turin Shroud," *New Scientist*, January 21, 1988, p. 22.
7. *Ibid.*
8. *Fidelity*, February 1989, p. 38.
9. *Ibid.*
10. *Shroud News*, No. 45, February 1988, p. 12; No. 47, June 1988, pp. 9-10.
11. *The Observer*, Vol. 20, No. 6, March 17-24, 1988, p. 8.
12. *Fidelity*, p. 42.
13. David Sox, *The Shroud Unmasked* (Basingstoke, England: The Lamp Press, 1988), p. 120.
14. M. S. Tite, "Turin Shroud," *Nature,* Vol. 332, April 7, 1988, p. 482.
15. *Nature*, Vol. 333, May 12, 1988, p. 110.
16. *Fidelity*, p. 42.
17. Sox, p. 133.
18. P. E. Damon, D. J. Donahue, *et al.*, "Radiocarbon dating of the Shroud of Turin," *Nature*, Vol. 337, February 16, 1989, p. 612.
19. Dr. Alan Adler in a lecture at the Holy Shroud Seminar Retreat, Esopus, NY, August 23, 1996.
20. *Tablet*, January 14, 1989, p. 36.
21. *Time*, April 20, 1998, p. 58.
22. Mary and Alan Whanger, *The Shroud of Turin*, p. 110.
23. *Nature*, February 16, 1989, p. 612.
24. Petrosillo & Marinelli, p. 62.
25. *Ibid.*, p. 64.
26. *Ibid.*, p. 66.
27. *Holy Shroud Guild Newsletter*, September 1989, p. 4.
28. Hoare, p. 11.
29. *Nature*, February 16, 1989, p. 612.
30. Sox, p. 137.
31. *Paris Match*, July 29, 1988, p. 4.
32. *Nature*, February 16, 1989, p. 612.

33. *National Geographic*, "Using Science to Date an Icon of Faith," February 1989.
34. *Nature*, February 16, 1989, p. 613.
35. *Ibid.*, p. 614.
36. *Il Giorno*, September 6, 1988.
37. *Shroud News*, October 1988, p. 7.
38. Remi Van Haelst, "Radiocarbon Dating the Shroud of Turin: A Critical Review of the Nature Report," p. 7.
39. *Il Giornale*, November 15, 1988, p. 9.
40. *Die Welt*, September 5, 1997.
41. Harry E. Gove, *Relic, Icon or Hoax?: Carbon Dating the Turin Shroud* (Philadelphia: Institute of Physics Publishing, 1996), p. 265.
42. *Reader's Digest* (Australian ed.), October 1989.
43. *La Stampa*, September 24, 1988.
44. *Shroud News*, June 1988, p. 11.
45. *The Tablet,* January 14, 1989, p. 37.
46. *La Stampa*, August 8, 1988.
47. *The Daily Telegraph*, March 25, 1989, p. 7.
48. *Shroud News*, No. 55, October 1989, p. 4.
49. *British Society for the Turin Shroud Newsletter*, January/February 1989, p. 4.
50. Meacham, p. 41.
51. Guscin, p. 72.
52. Van Haelst, p. 3.
53. *The Shroud Unmasked*, p. 138.
54. Meacham, p. 45.
55. *Ibid.*, p. 47.
56. *Ibid.*
57. *Ibid.*
58. *Ibid.*, p. 48.

## Chapter 10
## POST-1988 RESEARCH

1. *The Catholic World Report*, April 1993, p. 48.
2. *The Universe*, March 30, 1997.
3. *CRC*, September-October 1989, No. 223, p. 11, and March 1991, No. 237, pp. 5-6.
4. *Image*, Fall 1993, Vol. 1, No. 2, p. 3.
5. *Ibid.*
6. "Effects of Fires and Biofractionation of Carbon Isotopes on Results of Radiocarbon Dating of Old Textiles: The Shroud of Turin," in *Journal of Archaeological Science* (1996), vol. 23, pp. 109-121.
7. *Image,* Fall 1993, p. 7.
8. *National Catholic Register*, June 15, 1996, p. 9.

9. "Factors Affecting the Apparent Radiocarbon Age of Textiles: A Comment on 'Effects and Biofractionation of Carbon Isotopes on Results of Radiocarbon Dating of Old Textiles: The Shroud of Turin,'" by D. A. Kouznetsov *et al.*, in *Journal of Archaeological Science* (1996), Vol. 23, pp. 157-160.
10. John P. Jackson, Ph.D. and Keith Propp, Ph.D., "On the Evidence that the Radiocarbon Date of the Turin Shroud Was Significantly Affected by the 1532 Fire" (Colorado Springs, CO: Turin Shroud Center of Colorado, 1997), p. 1.
11. John P. Jackson, "Is the Image on the Shroud Due to a Process Heretofore Unknown to Modern Science?," *Shroud Spectrum International*, No. 34, March 1990, p. 5.
12. Dr. Leoncio A. Garza-Valdes, *The DNA of God?* (New York: Doubleday, 1999), p. 35.
13. *Ibid.*, 49.
14. *The Holy Shroud Guild Newsletter*, July 14, 1995, Vol. #2, No. 51, p. 3.
15. Garza-Valdes, p. 72.
16. John Allen, "The Shroud of Turin and Genetic Research," *The Tidings*, March 21, 1997, p. 15.
17. Garza-Valdes, p. 114.
18. *The Holy Shroud Guild Newsletter*, November 25, 1995, Vol. #3, No. 52, p. 1.
19. *Shroud Sources*, March 1993, p. 2.
20. *Ibid.*
21. Charlene Scott, *Holy Shroud Research Continues in Colorado* (Colorado Springs, CO: Sindone Press, 1994), p. 8.
22. Avinoam Danin, "Micro-Traces of Plants on the Shroud of Turin as Geographical Markers," International Scientific Symposium: "The Turin Shroud: Past, Present and Future," Turin, March 2-5, 2000 (Turin: Effatà Editrice, 2000), p. 496-497.
23. *The Catholic Transcript*, August 1997, p. 17.
24. *30 Days*, No. 3, 1995, p. 72.
25. Fr. Hilary Conti, O.S.B., *The Corporal and the Antimension* (unpublished manuscript), (Clifton, NJ: Holy Face Monastery, 1997).
26. *La Repubblica*, April 23, 1997, p. 22.

***If you have enjoyed this book, consider making your next selection from among the following . . .***

Holy Shroud and Four Visions. *Fr. O'Connell* . . . . . . . . . . . . . . . . . . . . . . . 2.00
Life Everlasting. *Garrigou-Lagrange, O.P.* . . . . . . . . . . . . . . . . . . . . . . . . 13.50
Mother of the Saviour/Our Int. Life. *Garrigou-Lagrange* . . . . . . . . . . . . . . . 13.50
Three Ages/Int. Life. *Garrigou-Lagrange. 2 vol. pb.* . . . . . . . . . . . . . . . . . . . 42.00
Ven. Francisco Marto of Fatima. *Cirrincione,* comp. . . . . . . . . . . . . . . . . . . . 1.50
Ven. Jacinta Marto of Fatima. *Cirrincione* . . . . . . . . . . . . . . . . . . . . . . . . . . 2.00
St. Philomena—The Wonder-Worker. *O'Sullivan* . . . . . . . . . . . . . . . . . . . . . 7.00
The Facts About Luther. *Msgr. Patrick O'Hare*. . . . . . . . . . . . . . . . . . . . . . . 16.50
Little Catechism of the Curé of Ars. *St. John Vianney.* . . . . . . . . . . . . . . . . . 6.00
The Curé of Ars—Patron Saint of Parish Priests. *Fr. B. O'Brien*. . . . . . . . . . . 5.50
Saint Teresa of Avila. *William Thomas Walsh* . . . . . . . . . . . . . . . . . . . . . . . . 21.50
Isabella of Spain: The Last Crusader. *William Thomas Walsh* . . . . . . . . . . . . . 20.00
Characters of the Inquisition. *William Thomas Walsh* . . . . . . . . . . . . . . . . . . 15.00
Blood-Drenched Altars—Cath. Comment. on Hist. Mexico. *Kelley* . . . . . . . . 20.00
The Four Last Things—Death, Judgment, Hell, Heaven. *Fr. von Cochem*. . . . 7.00
Confession of a Roman Catholic. *Paul Whitcomb*. . . . . . . . . . . . . . . . . . . . . . 1.50
The Catholic Church Has the Answer. *Paul Whitcomb* . . . . . . . . . . . . . . . . . . 1.50
The Sinner's Guide. *Ven. Louis of Granada* . . . . . . . . . . . . . . . . . . . . . . . . . 12.00
True Devotion to Mary. *St. Louis De Montfort* . . . . . . . . . . . . . . . . . . . . . . . . 8.00
Life of St. Anthony Mary Claret. *Fanchón Royer* . . . . . . . . . . . . . . . . . . . . . 15.00
Autobiography of St. Anthony Mary Claret. . . . . . . . . . . . . . . . . . . . . . . . . . 13.00
I Wait for You. *Sr. Josefa Menendez* . . . . . . . . . . . . . . . . . . . . . . . . . . . . . .75
Words of Love. *Menendez, Betrone, Mary of the Trinity*. . . . . . . . . . . . . . . . . 6.00
Little Lives of the Great Saints. *John O'Kane Murray* . . . . . . . . . . . . . . . . . . 18.00
Prayer—The Key to Salvation. *Fr. Michael Müller.* . . . . . . . . . . . . . . . . . . . . 7.50
Passion of Jesus and Its Hidden Meaning. *Fr. Groenings, S.J.*. . . . . . . . . . . . . 15.00
The Victories of the Martyrs. *St. Alphonsus Liguori* . . . . . . . . . . . . . . . . . . . 10.00
Canons and Decrees of the Council of Trent. *Transl. Schroeder* . . . . . . . . . . 15.00
Sermons of St. Alphonsus Liguori for Every Sunday. . . . . . . . . . . . . . . . . . . 16.50
A Catechism of Modernism. *Fr. J. B. Lemius* . . . . . . . . . . . . . . . . . . . . . . . . 5.00
Alexandrina—The Agony and the Glory. *Johnston*. . . . . . . . . . . . . . . . . . . . . 6.00
Life of Blessed Margaret of Castello. *Fr. William Bonniwell*. . . . . . . . . . . . . . 7.50
The Ways of Mental Prayer. *Dom Vitalis Lehodey* . . . . . . . . . . . . . . . . . . . . 14.00
Catechism of Mental Prayer. *Simler* . . . . . . . . . . . . . . . . . . . . . . . . . . . . . . 2.00
St. Francis of Paola. *Simi and Segreti* . . . . . . . . . . . . . . . . . . . . . . . . . . . . 8.00
St. Martin de Porres. *Giuliana Cavallini.* . . . . . . . . . . . . . . . . . . . . . . . . . . 12.50
The Story of the Church. *Johnson, Hannan, Dominica*. . . . . . . . . . . . . . . . . . 16.50
Hell Quizzes. *Radio Replies Press* . . . . . . . . . . . . . . . . . . . . . . . . . . . . . . . 1.50
Indulgence Quizzes. *Radio Replies Press* . . . . . . . . . . . . . . . . . . . . . . . . . . 1.50
Purgatory Quizzes. *Radio Replies Press* . . . . . . . . . . . . . . . . . . . . . . . . . . . 1.50
Virgin and Statue Worship Quizzes. *Radio Replies Press* . . . . . . . . . . . . . . . 1.50
Holy Eucharist: Our All. *Fr. Lukas Etlin*. . . . . . . . . . . . . . . . . . . . . . . . . . . . 2.00
Meditation Prayer on Mary Immaculate. *Padre Pio* . . . . . . . . . . . . . . . . . . . . 1.50
Little Book of the Work of Infinite Love. *de la Touche*. . . . . . . . . . . . . . . . . . 3.00
Textual Concordance of The Holy Scriptures. *Williams. pb.* . . . . . . . . . . . . . 35.00
Douay-Rheims Bible. *Paperbound* . . . . . . . . . . . . . . . . . . . . . . . . . . . . . . . 35.00
The Way of Divine Love. *Sister Josefa Menendez* . . . . . . . . . . . . . . . . . . . . 18.50
The Way of Divine Love. (pocket, unabr.). *Menendez*. . . . . . . . . . . . . . . . . . . 8.50
Mystical City of God—Abridged. *Ven. Mary of Agreda* . . . . . . . . . . . . . . . . . 18.50

Prices subject to change.

Moments Divine—Before the Blessed Sacrament. *Reuter* . . . . . . . . . . . . . . . 8.50
Miraculous Images of Our Lady. *Cruz* . . . . . . . . . . . . . . . . . . . . . . . . . . 20.00
Miraculous Images of Our Lord. *Cruz* . . . . . . . . . . . . . . . . . . . . . . . . . 13.50
Raised from the Dead. *Fr. Hebert*. . . . . . . . . . . . . . . . . . . . . . . . . . . . 16.50
Love and Service of God, Infinite Love. *Mother Louise Margaret* . . . . . . . . . 12.50
Life and Work of Mother Louise Margaret. *Fr. O'Connell* . . . . . . . . . . . . . . . 12.50
Autobiography of St. Margaret Mary. . . . . . . . . . . . . . . . . . . . . . . . . . . . 6.00
Thoughts and Sayings of St. Margaret Mary . . . . . . . . . . . . . . . . . . . . . . 5.00
The Voice of the Saints. *Comp. by Francis Johnston* . . . . . . . . . . . . . . . . . . 7.00
The 12 Steps to Holiness and Salvation. *St. Alphonsus*. . . . . . . . . . . . . . . . 7.50
The Rosary and the Crisis of Faith. *Cirrincione & Nelson* . . . . . . . . . . . . . . 2.00
Sin and Its Consequences. *Cardinal Manning* . . . . . . . . . . . . . . . . . . . . . . 7.00
St. Francis of Paola. *Simi & Segreti* . . . . . . . . . . . . . . . . . . . . . . . . . . . 8.00
Dialogue of St. Catherine of Siena. *Transl. Algar Thorold* . . . . . . . . . . . . . . 10.00
Catholic Answer to Jehovah's Witnesses. *D'Angelo* . . . . . . . . . . . . . . . . . . . 12.00
Twelve Promises of the Sacred Heart. (100 cards). . . . . . . . . . . . . . . . . . . . 5.00
Life of St. Aloysius Gonzaga. *Fr. Meschler* . . . . . . . . . . . . . . . . . . . . . . . 12.00
The Love of Mary. *D. Roberto* . . . . . . . . . . . . . . . . . . . . . . . . . . . . . . . 8.00
Begone Satan. *Fr. Vogl* . . . . . . . . . . . . . . . . . . . . . . . . . . . . . . . . . . . 3.00
The Prophets and Our Times. *Fr. R. G. Culleton*. . . . . . . . . . . . . . . . . . . . . 13.50
St. Therese, The Little Flower. *John Beevers* . . . . . . . . . . . . . . . . . . . . . . 6.00
St. Joseph of Copertino. *Fr. Angelo Pastrovicchi*. . . . . . . . . . . . . . . . . . . . 6.00
Mary, The Second Eve. *Cardinal Newman* . . . . . . . . . . . . . . . . . . . . . . . . 3.00
Devotion to Infant Jesus of Prague. *Booklet* . . . . . . . . . . . . . . . . . . . . . . .75
Reign of Christ the King in Public & Private Life. *Davies* . . . . . . . . . . . . . . . 1.25
The Wonder of Guadalupe. *Francis Johnston* . . . . . . . . . . . . . . . . . . . . . . . 7.50
Apologetics. *Msgr. Paul Glenn*. . . . . . . . . . . . . . . . . . . . . . . . . . . . . . . 10.00
Baltimore Catechism No. 1 . . . . . . . . . . . . . . . . . . . . . . . . . . . . . . . . . . 3.50
Baltimore Catechism No. 2 . . . . . . . . . . . . . . . . . . . . . . . . . . . . . . . . . . 4.50
Baltimore Catechism No. 3 . . . . . . . . . . . . . . . . . . . . . . . . . . . . . . . . . . 8.00
An Explanation of the Baltimore Catechism. *Fr. Kinkead*. . . . . . . . . . . . . . . . 16.50
Bethlehem. *Fr. Faber* . . . . . . . . . . . . . . . . . . . . . . . . . . . . . . . . . . . . 18.00
Bible History. *Schuster*. . . . . . . . . . . . . . . . . . . . . . . . . . . . . . . . . . . 13.50
Blessed Eucharist. *Fr. Mueller* . . . . . . . . . . . . . . . . . . . . . . . . . . . . . . . 9.00
Catholic Catechism. *Fr. Faerber*. . . . . . . . . . . . . . . . . . . . . . . . . . . . . . 7.00
The Devil. *Fr. Delaporte* . . . . . . . . . . . . . . . . . . . . . . . . . . . . . . . . . . 6.00
Dogmatic Theology for the Laity. *Fr. Premm* . . . . . . . . . . . . . . . . . . . . . . 20.00
Evidence of Satan in the Modern World. *Cristiani* . . . . . . . . . . . . . . . . . . . . 10.00
Fifteen Promises of Mary. (100 cards). . . . . . . . . . . . . . . . . . . . . . . . . . . 5.00
Life of Anne Catherine Emmerich. 2 vols. *Schmoeger* . . . . . . . . . . . . . . . . . 37.50
Life of the Blessed Virgin Mary. *Emmerich* . . . . . . . . . . . . . . . . . . . . . . . 16.50
Manual of Practical Devotion to St. Joseph. *Patrignani* . . . . . . . . . . . . . . . . 15.00
Prayer to St. Michael. (100 leaflets) . . . . . . . . . . . . . . . . . . . . . . . . . . . . 5.00
Prayerbook of Favorite Litanies. *Fr. Hebert* . . . . . . . . . . . . . . . . . . . . . . . 10.00
Preparation for Death. (Abridged). *St. Alphonsus* . . . . . . . . . . . . . . . . . . . . 8.00
Purgatory Explained. *Schouppe* . . . . . . . . . . . . . . . . . . . . . . . . . . . . . . 13.50
Purgatory Explained. (pocket, unabr.). *Schouppe* . . . . . . . . . . . . . . . . . . . . 9.00
Fundamentals of Catholic Dogma. *Ludwig Ott*. . . . . . . . . . . . . . . . . . . . . . . 21.00
Spiritual Conferences. *Faber* . . . . . . . . . . . . . . . . . . . . . . . . . . . . . . . . 15.00
Trustful Surrender to Divine Providence. *Bl. Claude* . . . . . . . . . . . . . . . . . . 5.00
Wife, Mother and Mystic. *Bessieres*. . . . . . . . . . . . . . . . . . . . . . . . . . . . 8.00
The Agony of Jesus. *Padre Pio*. . . . . . . . . . . . . . . . . . . . . . . . . . . . . . . 2.00

Prices subject to change.

The Life of Father De Smet. *Fr. Laveille, S.J.* . . . . . . . . . . 18.00
Hail Holy Queen (from *Glories of Mary*). *St. Alphonsus* . . . . . . . . 8.00
Novena of Holy Communions. *Lovasik* . . . . . . . . . . 2.00
Brief Catechism for Adults. *Cogan*. . . . . . . . . . 9.00
The Cath. Religion—Illus./Expl. for Child, Adult, Convert. *Burbach* . . . . . . . 9.00
Eucharistic Miracles. *Joan Carroll Cruz*. . . . . . . . . . 15.00
The Incorruptibles. *Joan Carroll Cruz* . . . . . . . . . . 13.50
Secular Saints: 250 Lay Men, Women & Children. *Cruz*. . . . . . . . . . 35.00
Pope St. Pius X. *F. A. Forbes* . . . . . . . . . . 8.00
St. Alphonsus Liguori. *Frs. Miller and Aubin* . . . . . . . . . . 16.50
Self-Abandonment to Divine Providence. *Fr. de Caussade, S.J.* . . . . . . . . . . 18.00
The Song of Songs—A Mystical Exposition. *Fr. Arintero, O.P.* . . . . . . . . . . 20.00
Prophecy for Today. *Edward Connor* . . . . . . . . . . 5.50
Saint Michael and the Angels. *Approved Sources* . . . . . . . . . . 7.00
Dolorous Passion of Our Lord. *Anne C. Emmerich*. . . . . . . . . . 16.50
Modern Saints—Their Lives & Faces, Book I. *Ann Ball*. . . . . . . . . . 18.00
Modern Saints—Their Lives & Faces, Book II. *Ann Ball* . . . . . . . . . . 20.00
Our Lady of Fatima's Peace Plan from Heaven. *Booklet*. . . . . . . . . . .75
Divine Favors Granted to St. Joseph. *Père Binet*. . . . . . . . . . 5.00
St. Joseph Cafasso—Priest of the Gallows. *St. John Bosco*. . . . . . . . . . 5.00
Catechism of the Council of Trent. *McHugh/Callan*. . . . . . . . . . 24.00
The Foot of the Cross. *Fr. Faber*. . . . . . . . . . 16.50
The Rosary in Action. *John Johnson* . . . . . . . . . . 9.00
Padre Pio—The Stigmatist. *Fr. Charles Carty* . . . . . . . . . . 15.00
Why Squander Illness? *Frs. Rumble & Carty*. . . . . . . . . . 2.50
The Sacred Heart and the Priesthood. *de la Touche* . . . . . . . . . . 9.00
Fatima—The Great Sign. *Francis Johnston* . . . . . . . . . . 8.00
Heliotropium—Conformity of Human Will to Divine. *Drexelius* . . . . . . . . . . 13.00
Charity for the Suffering Souls. *Fr. John Nageleisen* . . . . . . . . . . 16.50
Devotion to the Sacred Heart of Jesus. *Verheylezoon* . . . . . . . . . . 15.00
Who Is Padre Pio? *Radio Replies Press* . . . . . . . . . . 2.00
Child's Bible History. *Knecht*. . . . . . . . . . 5.00
The Stigmata and Modern Science. *Fr. Charles Carty* . . . . . . . . . . 1.50
The Life of Christ. 4 Vols. H.B. *Anne C. Emmerich*. . . . . . . . . . 60.00
St. Anthony—The Wonder Worker of Padua. *Stoddard*. . . . . . . . . . 5.00
The Precious Blood. *Fr. Faber* . . . . . . . . . . 13.50
The Holy Shroud & Four Visions. *Fr. O'Connell* . . . . . . . . . . 2.00
Clean Love in Courtship. *Fr. Lawrence Lovasik* . . . . . . . . . . 2.50
The Secret of the Rosary. *St. Louis De Montfort*. . . . . . . . . . 5.00
The History of Antichrist. *Rev. P. Huchede*. . . . . . . . . . 4.00
St. Catherine of Siena. *Alice Curtayne* . . . . . . . . . . 13.50
Where We Got the Bible. *Fr. Henry Graham* . . . . . . . . . . 6.00
Hidden Treasure—Holy Mass. *St. Leonard*. . . . . . . . . . 5.00
Imitation of the Sacred Heart of Jesus. *Fr. Arnoudt* . . . . . . . . . . 15.00
The Life & Glories of St. Joseph. *Edward Thompson*. . . . . . . . . . 15.00
Père Lamy. *Biver*. . . . . . . . . . 12.00
Humility of Heart. *Fr. Cajetan da Bergamo* . . . . . . . . . . 8.50
The Curé D'Ars. *Abbé Francis Trochu* . . . . . . . . . . 21.50
Love, Peace and Joy. (St. Gertrude). *Prévot* . . . . . . . . . . 7.00

# About the Author

Father Vittorio Guerrera was ordained in 1991; he is a priest of the Archdiocese of Hartford. Besides degrees in psychology and sociology, Father received a Master of Divinity degree from Christ the King Seminary in East Aurora, New York, and a Licentiate in Sacred Theology from the Pontifical Gregorian University in Rome.

The author first learned of the Shroud when a teenager, and he began a serious study of it following the controversial 1988 Carbon-14 testing. He attended the 1996 Shroud Symposium in Esopus, New York and the Third International Congress for Shroud Studies in Turin in 1998. He was also present during the exposition of the Shroud in the Jubilee Year 2000. Father was a contributing columnist for *The Catholic Transcript* and currently is the interim Director of Formation for the Permanent Diaconate Program for the Archdiocese of Hartford. He has been inducted into Marquis' *Who's Who in the East* and has written several books, including *Let the Children Come to Me: Homilies for Children*.